Bringing Out the Untold Life

Recollections of Mildred Reid Grant Gray

*Canadian Morse Code Operator Chronicles Nine Decades
In Historic Cape Breton Fishing Village*

An Oral History
Related to Claire E. Scheuren

Highlights of Gabarus History
By Claire E. Scheuren

ZEITGEIST WEST
PUBLISHING

Published in the United States by Zeitgeist West.
Visit us on the web: www.zeitgeistwest.com

Photographs used by permission, from the collections of Mildred Grant Gray Family; Lillian and Kathy Harriss Family; Rising Tide Expeditions (www.risingtideexpeditions.com); Jocelyn Bethune; Aerial Photograph of Gabarus Village by Warren Gordon Photographic http://gordonphoto.com/; Nova Scotia Archives: *Gabarus. Red Cross Caravan, 6 August 1920;* NSA, Helen Creighton fonds, Album 12 no. 68; Beaton Institute: *Beryl Markham's Plane. 1936.* Photographer Unknown. Item Number 89-1216-19390. Beaton Institute, Cape Breton University; *Ice Boat, Second Lake Gabarus. 1942.* Photographer Unknown. Item Number 89-1216-19424. Beaton Institute, Cape Breton University; *Grant Property-Waiting for Mailman. 1944.* Photographer Unknown. Item Number 89-1216-19407. Beaton Institute, Cape Breton University; *Shipwreck of Iceland II in Fourchu. February 26, 1967* Photo by Abbass, Used with permission from Abbass Studios; *Shipwreck of Marshall Frank. February 18, 1949.* Photo by Vince Riley. From Cape Breton Post.

Poem on dedication page is reprinted with permission from Many Rivers Press, www.davidwhyte.com. David Whyte, Looking Back At Night, Where Many Rivers Meet 1996 ©Many Rivers Press, Langley, Washington.

Drawings of two-masted schooner and shallop by Benjamin B. Schwartz
Map of Gabarus Village by David Fitzsimmons

Copyright © Claire E. Scheuren, 2013
All Rights Reserved

The author has made every effort to locate and contact all of the holders of copyright to material in this book.

Printed in the United States of America
Library of Congress Catalogue-in-Publication Data

Gray, Mildred Reid Grant Gray 1920-
Scheuren, Claire E. 1947-

Bringing Out The Untold Life: *Recollections of Mildred Reid Grant Gray Related to Claire E. Scheuren*
Highlights of Gabarus History by Claire E. Scheuren
Includes Introduction, Highlights of Gabarus History and Bibliographical References
ISBN # 978-0-9796921-1-6 (pbk.)
ISBN # 978-0-9796921-3-0 (hc.)
ISBN # 978-0-9796921-2-3 (ebook)
Mildred Reid Grant Gray (Canada) – Oral History
1. Gabarus, Cape Breton, Nova Scotia-History
2. Cape Breton folklore
Book design and Gabarus and area maps by Carla Turco
First Edition

Printed from responsibly managed forests: The printer of this book, Lightning Source, is certified by the Sustainable Forestry Initiative® that documents responsible environmental behavior for today and for future generations utilizing a Chain of Custody (CoC) accounting system that tracks wood fiber through the different stages of production. For publishers, and ultimately consumers, CoC ensures the integrity of the paper supply chain and that the paper used in Lightning Source® printed books are from responsibly managed forests. SFI® Certificate Number: PwC-SFICOC-345 SFI-00980.

Dedicated to the noble citizens of Gabarus, past and present.

…Now, by the small body of my sleeping son
the hidden river in my chest flows with his
and I time my speech to the rhythm of his breath
joining my night with his, singing his night song
as if those waters underground
were secret rivers washing through the soul,
bringing out the untold life
which is the stream he'll join in growing old,
in silent hours when his sureness
of his self recedes. There he'll find
the rest between the solid notes
that makes the song worthwhile…

David Whyte

Table of Contents

Introduction 1
Mildred Reid Grant Gray 7

ANCESTRAL FAMILY AND COMMUNITY
Early Gabarus Settlers 11
Great-grandparents William and Mary Grant 12
Crossing the Mira I 13
Ruth West and William Sutherland 17
My Father's Parents Captain John and Emma Armstrong Grant 18
My Mother's Parents Albert and Elizabeth Grant Reid's Three Children 20
Grandpa Reid and His Superstitions 22
Grammy Reid 23
Grammy Grant 25
Crossing the Mira II 27
My Childhood Home 29
My Father Wiley Ormiston Grant 30
My Mother Elsie Reid Grant 32
Elsie's Long Life 33
My Big Sister Freda 34
The Boston States 37

MEMORIES OF THE LAST CENTURY IN GABARUS
FROM HORSE-DRAWN SLEIGH TO INTERNET
Captain John Grant in the Era of Sail 49
Ship Building 51
Gull Cove 52
Turn of the Century 53
Old Fashioned Values 55
1920s Gabarus 56
Pound Party 58
Down and Out in Gabarus 59
Healthy Eating and Hard Work 60
Breakfast, Lunch, and Pies 61
Barter for Butter 62
Hooking Mats 63
Pre-electric World 64
Seven Stores in Gabarus 66
Grant Store 67
Puncheon of Molasses 72
Coal and Kerosene 73

Dan and Myrtle Stewart 74
Grant and Reid Undertakers 75
Orange Lodge 77
Mid-Winter Orange Drive 78
Doctor in the Village 79
Mail Delivery and Early Automobiles in Gabarus 81
Outings to Sydney and Vidol Hotel 82
School Days 83
Childhood Games 86
Earthquake of 1929 88
Cutting the Ice 89
Prohibition Adventures 91
Music and Community Life 92
Dance on Crazy Horse Bridge 94
Church Life in Gabarus 95
Christmas Concert, Highlight of the Winter 99
Our Family Christmas 101
Birds and Bees 103
Best Friends 105
Ice Skating at Night 107
Thrilling Ice Boat 109
Gabarus-Louisbourg Ferry 111
Lighthouse and Landmarks 113
Swordfishing in the 1930s 114
Elsie Caught Wiley a Swordfish From the Window 115
Lobster Factory 116
Fishing Changes in My Lifetime 117
Summer of 16 Ice Cream Parlor 119
Provincial Exams and Peroxide 120
Pet Monkey 122
The Day Grandpa Captain Grant Died 123
Gloom Over the Community 124
World War II 125
Buzz and Beryl 128
Wartime Wedding 129
Lobster Buyer Business 134
Selling The Store 135
Living History 137

ONE WOMAN 911
Christina Grant and the History of Morse Code in Gabarus 141
How I Became the Morse Code Operator 143
Gabarus Telegraph Office 145
Telegrams and Bad News 148
Doctor and Vet Calls 150

1950s Cow Gone Wild 151
Shipwrecks and Salvation.. 152
The Wreck of the Marshall Frank in 1949.. 153
Iceland II Goes Aground in Fourchu... 154
Interview with Spray Paint 155
The Start of the Switchboard 156
Switchboard and Social Service 157
Dying Family Friend... 158
Two Young Lives Lost 159
Destiny Calls 160
Reluctant Retirement 161

FAMILY AND THE FUTURE
Family Picnics 165
18 Minutes... 166
Mi'kmaw Picnic Basket 167
My Husband Duncan Gray and Our Family 168
Duncan's Best Fudge Recipe Ever 170
The Day Duncan Died.. 171
My Children 173
Staying Physically and Emotionally Flexible 174
Nine Decades of Changes to Land and Sea 176
What's Next.. 178
Secrets to Longevity 179
Summing Up 181
What is the Future of Gabarus?... 183

HIGHLIGHTS OF GABARUS HISTORY
Highlights of Gabarus History 187
Cod, the Wonder Fish 193
Chaloupe, Shallop 195
Capbreton to Cape Breton 197
How Gabarus Got Its Name: A Bay, a Lake, and a Fishing Port.................. 197
Sister Settlements: Gabarus and Louisbourg.. 200
A Temperate, Industrious and Thriving People 200
Treaty of Utrecht in 1713.. 201
Île Royale: Front Door of Canada 204
First Siege of Louisbourg.. 204
Aix-la-Chapelle in 1748 and the Birthplace of the American Nation 206
Second Siege of Louisbourg... 207
Cape Breton, British Colony 209
19th and 20th Century Developments.. 210
Barachois 213
Scottish Settlers 214
Methodism in Gabarus 216

Sydney Steel Plant and Gabarus Wilderness Area 217
Center of the 20th Century Communications Revolution 218
The Spelling of Gabarus 222
Aerial Photograph of Gabarus Village 225
Drawing of Gabarus Village 226
Map of Gabarus and Surrounding Area 227

BIBLIOGRAPHY AND ACKNOWLEDGEMENTS
Endnotes 228
Select Bibliography for Highlights of Gabarus History 235
Acknowledgements 240
Claire E. Scheuren 243

Introduction

Mildred Gray is acknowledged as the last surviving government-employed Morse Code operator and one of the last surviving manual switchboard operators in the Canadian Maritime provinces. From the 1940s through the 1970s, Mrs. Gray was a one-woman 911, information and referral service, spiritual advisor, and companion to people giving birth and people dying. Now we need multiple institutions to do what Mrs. Gray and the other telegraph and switchboard operators did. Currently, Mrs. Gray resides in her lifetime home of Gabarus Village on Cape Breton Island in Nova Scotia, Canada where she is a direct descendant of its 18th century European settlers.

Bringing Out The Untold Life: Recollections of Mildred Reid Grant Gray presents Mrs. Gray's recollections of events and experiences over the nine decades of her life. This book contains her oral history, my verbatim notes of over two hundred conversations with Mildred Gray who is my neighbor and friend. Maps and numerous historic and family photographs are also included.

Mrs. Gray has an extraordinary memory for detail. How many of us can cite the birthdates of our great-grandparents? Her detailed recollections bring us close to seeing the poignant simplicity of another time. I hope that details in this book will be enjoyed by Mrs. Gray and her family and neighbors, community historians, ethnographers and anthropologists and other scholars of civic life, communication, Cape Breton and Canadian history. Mrs. Gray's recollections show a significant system of meanings in the lives of a very special cultural group.

Mrs. Gray's personal story reflects the character and culture of the Gabarus community and the neighboring communities of Fourchu, Framboise, and Gabarus Lake. At one level this is a personal and family history with dates and details that may not appear to be relevant or interesting to people who live outside the immediate area. But when we look deeper we see the universal human stories of families striving to survive and thrive in difficult conditions.

We see how shared experience can bring out the best in people. We see the flow of history and both the development and the retreat of population and local commerce. Overall, community abides, and the citizens of Gabarus remain uncommonly unified in their expression of caring, authentic hospitality and service to each other.

Advocates for world peace may also take heed. No community is without conflict and disagreement, but in Gabarus, difficulties are more readily addressed and absorbed in an ocean of community goodwill. The emotionally embedded proscription against back biting and gossip has fostered healthier, more functional, relationships over the generations and centuries.

Gabarus is a place both beautiful and real. The windswept rocky shore contrasts with the warmth of community. As Mrs. Gray points out, the old values still live here. Wherever you live in the world, you can learn about how to live a good life by following the story of Mrs. Gray and her community of Gabarus in guiding us all to be useful, compassionate and honorable. You will see that Mrs. Gray and her family and neighbors, whether they are Methodist or not, live by John Wesley's directive to "Do all the good you can. By all the means you can… As long as ever you can!"

Sound idyllic? It is. In Gabarus, there is something perfectly wonderful about the sameness of simple things, the changing character and color of the sea, birds and boats to watch, companionable neighbors who go about their lives outside your windows, but can always be called upon for a cup of tea, a kind word, or any kind of practical assistance.

This is the story of a fine woman and her family who live in the near 300-year-old historic and beautiful fishing village of Gabarus, on the east coast of Cape Breton Island in Nova Scotia, Canada, described in a recent news story in the Toronto Globe and Mail as "a postcard-perfect slice of seaside Canadiana."[1]

Bringing Out The Untold Life is also a story of a place and a people at the hub of history.

Highlights of Gabarus History follow Mrs. Gray's recollections. In the hope of providing a grounded context for Mrs. Gray's recollections, I started with Mildred Gray's memories and her excellent recall of what she had heard of the days before her time. I read much of the historical literature about Cape Breton, Louisbourg, the history of the Mi'kmaq[2] native people, early explorers, cod fishing, the immigration of Scots, the early Methodists, and the days of sail. You will see that I have relied extensively on historian Robert J. Morgan's books on Cape Breton history, Rev. George and Mrs. Lavery's book on Gabarus history specifically, Ronald Caplan's interviews in Cape Breton's Magazine, Professor Brian Tennyson's histories and compilations of the early documents and commentaries, and the research of community historians Tim Menk and Gene Kersey on Gabarus's name, and other points of interest.

I hope that both Mrs. Gray's Recollections and the Highlights of Gabarus History will inform and excite the imagination of anyone interested in the story of Gabarus and its noble citizens, past and present, to whom this book is dedicated.

Mildred Reid Grant Gray has generously shared her stories here. They bring to life what can no longer be seen or experienced directly. Yet her recollections show us all how our way of life today can still be firmly set on that foundation of the past. According to the McCord Museum of Canadian History the Mi'kmaq have a word for this: elaptog, "prints left by someone who has passed by."[3] Let us walk together with Mrs. Gray in the footprints of those who came before us.

Claire E. Scheuren
Tucson, Arizona
December 2013

Recollections of
Mildred Reid Grant Gray

An Oral History

Mildred Reid Grant Gray

TOP ROW LEFT TO RIGHT
TEACHERS ANNIE JOHNSON AND RITA REID
BOTTOM ROW LEFT TO RIGHT
FREDA GRANT (SECOND FROM LEFT), **JANET MACDONALD** (FIFTH FROM LEFT), **MILDRED GRANT, AGE 3** (SIXTH FROM LEFT).
CA. 1923. MILDRED GRAY FAMILY PHOTOGRAPH.
USED WITH PERMISSION.

I don't like fiction. I don't like fantasy. I like true things. For me, reality has always been rewarding. I have seen death, loss, shipwrecks, grieving parents, fatherless children, poverty and pain. My own beloved husband was taken from me violently and by surprise. I have dealt with all of it. I have also experienced great joys, loving family, happy memories, world travel, wonderful children and grandchildren, and important and meaningful work. I have been blessed with human sensitivity, and a resilient, energetic and hardworking character. Now I am the last surviving government-employed Morse Code operator and one of the last surviving manual switchboard operators in the Maritime Provinces. This is my story.

When you live over ninety years you see and remember, and I have memories since I was five years old. In those nine decades of my life, I have seen a lot of changes. Time goes by so fast. My memories are very vivid, as if it was yesterday.

I was born at home on May 13, 1920, the second of three children of Elsie and Wiley Grant. I was born in the house that my brother Kenneth lives in now. That was our family home.

Introduction   7

As a child, I was very fortunate to be surrounded by family. All four of my grandparents and both great-grandmothers lived within a few houses of ours in Gabarus Village on the island of Cape Breton, Nova Scotia. Many of my aunts, uncles and cousins also lived nearby. Over 100 years, four generations of Grants worked in the family general store: myself, my father Wiley, his father Captain John Grant and his father William Grant.

My grandparents all lived very close. They were all very different. I got an education from each of them. You learn different things from different people. Their values were pretty much the same. They all felt that Christianity and the church were the center of their lives. They truly believed in, and practiced, ideas of Christian living. They lived simple lives. Everyone helped each other. That type of living. They gave what they had, maybe just advice, but they were always giving. They were mild mannered, happy people. I was fortunate. We had the store too, so we had a little more than some.

Two of my grandparents and two of my great-grandparents died when I was nine and ten, but both my father's father and my mother's mother lived on into my adult life. Both my grandfather Albert Reid and my great-grandmother Mary Grant died in 1929. Mary Grant was 101 when she died. In those days it was unusual for someone to live over 100. My great-grandmother on my mother's side, Nancy Sutherland Reid (her husband's name was William too), was also living when I was born. She had dementia or Alzheimer's, and she didn't know us. She was eighty-seven years old when I was born. She was afraid of thunder and lightning storms. In storms, if she was outside, she would put a shawl on her head and run home to Grammy Reid's house which is where she lived before she died in 1929 at the age of ninety-six. Grammy Emma Grant died in 1930 at the age of seventy-three. Her husband, my grandfather Captain John Grant, was eighty-one when he died nine years later in 1939. Grammy Elizabeth Reid died in 1944 at the age of seventy-eight.

ANCESTRAL FAMILY AND COMMUNITY

Early Gabarus Settlers

My ancestor William Bagnell was one of the first settlers in Gabarus. He had been an officer in Wolfe's army when they defeated the French at Louisbourg in 1758. Another ancestor was Townsend. They were among the first settlers in Louisbourg, and they married into Gabarus families. The Ayles, Hardy and Stacey families came from Newfoundland in the 1700s.

Gabarus is connected to the history of what happened in Louisbourg. There are graves over by Harbour Point from colonial times. At that time, there was a hospital for soldiers on Rouse Point. It was used by the French and the English in the two takings of Louisbourg. Later the land on Rouse Point was owned by William Henry MacGillivary, and then Mrs. Reid owned it. When she died, Townsend owned it. Mr. MacGillivary was married to a Stacey. Their daughter had divorced and lived with them and looked after them. This was in the 1930s. She taught Sunday school for many years when I was little. When her parents died she married a minister from Massachusetts named Reid. The land was in the middle of Rouse Island. There is a place behind it that people called Angel's Retreat. That was where the hospital was. There was a mark chiseled in a rock that showed where it was, but there is nothing left of the hospital. There are probably a lot of artifacts under the ground there. My grandson Grant used a metal detector over there, but it could only read 4 inches. It's not strong enough to go down far. He found some little bullets, but not much else.

Mary MacDonald Grant and William Grant at home in Gabarus. ca. 1915. Mildred Gray Family Photograph. Used with permission.

Great-grandparents William and Mary Grant

I had Grants on both sides of my family. I had two great-grandfathers who were Grants. Sam Grant, my mother's grandfather, was first cousin to William Grant, my father's grandfather. Sam Grant ran a hotel and a store and a post office at Lever Hill. William Grant started the Grant Store in Gabarus Village.

My great-grandmother on my father's side was Margaret Ann "Mary" MacDonald Grant. Her father John MacDonald [1802-1861] was born in 1802 on the Isle of Mull in the Hebrides Islands west of Scotland, and he came to West Bay, Nova Scotia. Her mother Ruth Sutherland [1804-1871] was born in St. Peters [Nova Scotia] in 1804. Great Grammy Grant was a nice lady, a big woman.

Great Grammy Mary was born October 18, 1828 in Grand Anse. She was married to William Grant who was born June 19, 1826 in St. Peters and died in Gabarus in 1916 at the age of ninety. They both ended their lives in Gabarus. My great-grandfather William Grant had the store, and they also had the hotel, which was more of a boarding house since the family lived there. The Grant Hotel was across the street from the current Gabarus Post Office.

In those days we needed a hotel in Gabarus, because it took so long to get back into town on horseback. Salespeople, like the Morse's Tea salesman, would come on the train from Halifax to Sydney and then come in a horse and wagon to sell things to the store. Sometimes they would come on the ferry between Gabarus and Louisbourg. They would stay at Grant's Hotel all night. Great-Grammy Grant would feed the horse. The salesmen would also take orders for things they had in Halifax, and then Grandpa Grant would go there [to Halifax] and pick them up in his vessel.

12   Bringing Out the Untold Life

Crossing the Mira I

My great-grandparents William [1826-1916] and Mary Grant [1828-1929] originally came from West Bay [Nova Scotia]. Both Mary and William's families were from Scotland, then New Brunswick. In 1847, they walked from Grant's Hills outside of Gabarus to Sydney [26 miles/42 km] to get married in the Anglican Church. At that time, the minister was a traveling minister, based in Sydney. Mary was 19 at the time, and William was 21. The bridge across the Mira wasn't built then, so they went across on a raft. It was in early April. According to family lore, Mary lost one of her shoes, but then later found it. After they were married, they walked all the way back and moved to their land grant, what is now called Grant's Hills, a wooded area that was named for them, about 5-10 miles from Gabarus Village.

Recently a friend of mine was out walking on Grant's Hills and saw a hemlock tree that is not native to the area. The tree is right near the rocks showing where their house stood. There are two kinds of hemlock, a poisonous shrub or a tree, and they both have to be planted by hand. It doesn't propagate on its own. My friend brought me a piece of the root which was rotten, a stump, and we had it examined by the Department of Lands and Forests. They confirmed that it would have had to be planted by human hands. I think my great-grandmother Mary must have planted it around the mid 1800s. I like to think that she planted it. It makes me feel more connected to her.

They lived in Grant's Hills in the winter and Gabarus in the summer where my great-grandfather William had established his store. They called Gabarus "The Harbour." Their home in Gabarus Village was across from the existing post office. At that time it was a very big house. The front of the house was right on the highway, but it has since been torn off. Now it is mostly what was the kitchen of the old house.

William and Mary had nine children, most of whom died young from tuberculosis. One of their children was my grandfather Captain John Grant, my father's father. My great uncle George who was born on October 29, 1864 had TB. George was the first to go to Arizona to improve his health. He was studying to be a minister. When he came home to die they landed him on the back of the beach, as far away from people as possible.

Everyone was very careful not to get too close, afraid of becoming infected. It was not long after that he died at only 32 leaving his wife Theresa [b. January 27, 1872] from Louisbourg, who was a nurse. She lived with Grammy quite a while. After George died, Theresa married his brother Abraham who was born on January 1, 1867, and they had three boys: Howard, Emerson, and George. They were my father's generation. Sadly, Theresa died of TB herself at the age of 32.

When my family members traveled to Arizona, they went by train. The railroads to Tucson were just starting when they first went there. My family went to Arizona to help their TB, but the main reason they chose Tucson was because of our cousin John Breck Grant. He lived in Tucson and worked for Southern Pacific as a construction engineer. He sent money to his relatives in Gabarus and encouraged them to come to Arizona. As a hobby, he was supposed to have had a buffalo farm. One of my great-grandfather William's brothers was John Breck Grant's father. He was also from Cape Breton, West Bay, near St. Peters. Grant Road, a main road in Tucson, Arizona is named after my cousin John Breck Grant.

At one time or another, my great uncle Abraham Grant and all of his children lived in Tucson, Arizona. Uncle Abe, Howard, George, and Jimmy are buried at the Evergreen Cemetery there. Emerson is buried in Vancouver. George and Howard Grant continued to live in Tucson where Howard was murdered in 1961 by one of [Jimmy] Hoffa's men. His death left his wife Dorothy and three boys. When he was alive, Howard and Dorothy used to go back and forth from Tucson to Gabarus every five years. They had a son named Jimmy. They were good friends with my parents. Howard was the President of the Teamsters Union in Arizona. We heard that his murder started a rebellion against Hoffa's rule. I remember that Howard's wife Dorothy was a great piano player, and she may have moved to California after Howard was killed.

Some of my great-grandparents' [William and Mary Grant's] other children were Absolom V. Grant who died on April 3, 1886 at age 29, and Mary Edith Grant, who died in 1900 at age 29. They both died of TB. The other children were Sam, William, Margaret, and daughter Jane, who was married to Tom Bagnell. Jane was only 25 when she died; and Nelson was 14 when he died. The only children of my great-grandparents who lived a long time were Abraham and my grandfather, Captain John Grant.

LEFT TO RIGHT
ABRAHAM GRANT, WILEY GRANT WITH DOG, ALEX CAMPBELL, LORENA CAMPBELL, EMMA AND JOHN GRANT. CA. 1896. MILDRED GRAY FAMILY PHOTOGRAPH. USED WITH PERMISSION.

TB used to run in families. At the time, people lived together in fairly close quarters, and sanitary conditions weren't the greatest. A lot of young people had TB in those days. They would catch it from each other. There was TB in Gabarus until the 1930s-1940s when antibiotics became available. None of my immediate family had it. Some people had it and got over it. In 1925 TB went through another family, and their children died young.

Even though Mary and William had nine children, they still had room to board women from out of the village who came to Gabarus to work in the lobster factory. These girls would work for board. The girls had to make the bread, and my great-grandmother Mary was very particular. They had to knead it 100 times. The women were young, 18-20; they worked in the factory until they got married. Many of the young women married men from Gabarus.

When Great Grammy Mary's husband William died in 1916, her son Abraham stayed home with her. Abraham took over the store right down the street, and went to Arizona around 1929 or 1930 with his son Howard. Later, my great-grandmother Mary had no money, so she went to live with my Grammy Grant. I remember her knitting in her chair. My niece still has the chair.

Ancestral Family and Community 15

I was nine when Great Grammy Grant died, so I didn't really get to know her well. I do remember her though. I was told by the family that she couldn't write, but when I was in Salt Lake City, Utah, looking at genealogical records, I saw her signature on their wedding license. I know my great-grandfather used to hold the Bible up to the lamp and read it to her. Perhaps she could have read it herself.

Ruth West and William Sutherland

I would love to find out more about my great-great-great-grandmother Ruth West. I do know that she was married to William Sutherland and that they lived in West Bay and had thirteen children including my great-great-grandmother Peggy Sutherland [b.1795- mother of William Grant]. Ruth West became a midwife and drowned in the River Tillard in River Bourgeois on her way to deliver a baby. They were married in 1791 in Guysborough, and she died about 1821. That much I do know. But what we would like to confirm is the story that when she was a child, the Indians captured her from her family in what is now Long Island, New York. We had always heard that her family "owned Long Island." Ruth West was kidnapped, captured by the Indians, and brought to West Bay, Cape Breton, where my great-great-great-grandfather had a store. An Indian brought her in to shop when she was fourteen. That is how they met. William was born in 1754 at Wick, Scotland, so he would have been thirty-seven when they married.

My Father's Parents Captain John and Emma Armstrong Grant

My father's parents Captain John [1843-1940] and Emma Armstrong Grant [1856-1930] had four children: Ella, Lorena, my father Wiley, and Ernest. The first child was Ella who was born on February 11, 1879. She married Bert Plunkett and lived in Massachusetts for most of her adult life. Aunt Ella and Uncle Bert never had any children. Aunt Ella played a significant role in my life. I'll tell you a lot more about her later.

Second was my Aunt Cassie Lorena who was born on October 16, 1881. She married Alex Campbell, and they lived in Sydney. After Alex became ill with throat cancer, they moved back to Gabarus from Sydney. I remember the day Aunt Lorena, my Uncle Alex and their two boys came back to Gabarus. It was my fifth birthday, May 13, 1925. I was sitting on a well box cover when they went by in my father's horse and wagon. In those days, there was no cure for throat cancer, and he was coming home to die. They had traveled from Sydney to Louisbourg on the train and then took the ferry to Gabarus. My father had picked them up at the ferry that came in at the old government wharf near the lighthouse. My father took them home to stay with Grammy and Captain Grant. Uncle Alex was only in his late twenties. The doctor in Gabarus helped as much as he could. His care was a lot like hospice today, at home, with family taking care of him with the doctor helping. He died in Gabarus that year and is buried in Lakeview Cemetery.

Then Aunt Lorena was a young widow with two children, and she and her two little boys, my first cousins, Ernie and Kenneth, stayed with my Grammy and Captain Grant for two or three years after that. My Aunt Lorena gave me a book that I have never forgotten, Tim and the Twins. I always loved the little stories in that book.

Later, Aunt Lorena and the boys moved to Cambridge, Massachusetts, to be near my Aunt Ella. Aunt Lorena went to work at S.S. Pierce, the fancy grocery store in Boston. To make extra money, Aunt Lorena also made food to sell there, and Ella helped them out quite a bit.

CAPTAIN JOHN GRANT TAKEN BY ELLA GRANT PLUNKETT. CA. 1929. MILDRED GRAY FAMILY PHOTOGRAPH. USED WITH PERMISSION.

Aunt Ella and Bert especially helped with the boys. Every summer Uncle Bert took the boys to their cottage in Maine to go fishing.

After they grew up, both of my cousins served in the American army during the Second World War. After only three months in Italy, Ernest was killed. That was a huge loss, and Aunt Lorena died not long after, in 1949, of asthma and a heart condition. My cousin Kenneth was in the Medical Corps, and when he came back he became the manager of the electric department of Jordan Marsh.

Kenneth was the buyer and traveled all over to places like Yugoslavia and Czechoslovakia to buy lights. Sometimes we saw him when he went on buying trips. Every summer, he came to see our grandparents, as long as they were alive. Kenneth and his wife Claire had six children, two girls and four boys, and five are still living and often come to see me. The oldest is now seventy. For most of their childhood they lived in Quincy, Massachusetts, and then Kenneth was transferred to Philadelphia which is where he lived when he died three years ago at the age of ninety-two or ninety-three. His wife Claire died ten years before him.

My father Wiley was the third born in November 10, 1884, and Uncle Ernest was the youngest of the four children. Uncle Ernest was born on October 27, 1892, and he died in 1962, three years before my father died in 1965. Ernie was in the army in the First World War. When he came home, he went to college in Halifax and worked for the Department of Veterans Affairs. We used to see him when he came to Sydney for his work. Uncle Ernest had four very accomplished children. One is eighty-three now. One daughter was married to a man who served in the Nova Scotia Legislature, and another was a director of Canadian Health. His grandchildren still call and come to visit.

My Mother's Parents Albert and Elizabeth Grant Reid's Three Children

My grandfather (my mother's father) Albert Reid was born in Gabarus on January 13, 1860. His parents were Nancy "Annie" Sutherland [1833-1929] and William Reid [1829-1914]. His parents were married in 1854.

Albert and Mary Elizabeth "Lizzie" Grant Reid had three children: John, Herb, and my mother Elsie. First born was John who was born on December 5, 1887; second born was Herb born on September 23, 1889, and my mother Elsie, born on September 26, 1892, was the youngest.

John married Jemima Payne who came from Newfoundland. John became a Justice of the Peace like my father, and they were in the undertaking business together. Uncle John and Aunt Jemima Reid lived on Gull Cove Road. They had four children. One died of pneumonia at 9 months of age; the others were Herb, Jean, and Elsie.

Our families were very close. Aunt Jemima was about my mother's age, and she and my mother spent a lot of time together. They were the best of friends, and I was good friends with my cousins Jean and Elsie. Jean was two years older than I was, and she was very lively, a lot of fun. We started school together, and were in regular contact until she died. Jean became a nurse, Elsie was a stenographer, and Herb was a minister in the United Church. My daughter Nancy went out west to Alberta with my cousin Herb when she was in her early twenties.

I have a lot of memories of Aunt Jemima including our annual trips to Sydney. So many memories. When I was little, Aunt Jemima and Grammy Reid were planting potatoes just down the road from where they lived. Jean and I were with them. Grammy Reid's cat Martha followed them down to where they were planting. While they were at the potato patch she had three kittens. Aunt Jemima brought them home in her apron with Martha running behind. Everyone wore aprons then.

LEFT TO RIGHT
JOHN, ELSIE AND HERB REID WITH PARENTS ALBERT AND ELIZABETH. CA. 1907. MILDRED GRAY FAMILY PHOTOGRAPH.
USED WITH PERMISSION.

Uncle Herb became a fisherman. He had a lot of love interests when he was young, including the school teachers who came to Gabarus, but he never married. I don't think my grandmother was approving of his girlfriends, and she didn't want him to leave home.

Uncle Herb was a very good person, kind. He loved children. He would give me five cents for finding the first dandelion in the spring. He lived at home with his parents until he died at only fifty-seven during surgery. That was 1947, the first time I went to see Aunt Ella in Boston, and it was also my first time in an airplane when I had to fly back to Sydney after he died on June 7th.

Grandpa Albert Reid was a fisherman. He would fish codfish and mackerel and probably some lobster. At that time, there was really no competition in the fishing industry. Everybody did the same thing, and people helped each other. Fishermen would help each other launch boats or anything that was needed. No jealousy or anything like that. People knew how to get along. To this day, there is a verbal agreement between the lobster fishermen in Fourchu and Gabarus to never cross each other's lines.

Grandpa Reid and His Superstitions

I never saw my Grandpa Reid smile; my cousin told me he never did. From what I remember and what I have heard, he was a very quiet, stone sober man. Grandpa Reid was active in the church and would give sermons, so he must have had deeply held religious beliefs. I was only nine years old when he died in 1929, so I never had a chance to know him that well. But I have heard that he was quite superstitious. He would never take a woman out with him on his fishing boat, and no one was allowed on the boat in grey mittens. They had to wear white mittens, and there was no whistling on the boat either. Looking out at the new moon through glass was bad luck. My mother Elsie would say "There is new moon!" But she would never look at it through a window. She would go outside and look at it. Even yet, one of my first cousins from the Reid side is very superstitious.

In my childhood, Grammy Reid was also superstitious. There was another woman who would scare people by prophesying what would happen in the future. She was the widow of the old lighthouse keeper at Guyon Island who had drowned. She lived down at the Cape which is about six miles from Gabarus, about a mile past Gull Cove. She used to walk back and forth until the early 1950s. She would tell you something would happen, and sometimes it would. I don't think she wanted to scare people, but she did. At night, she walked alone with a candle lantern.

Grammy Reid

My grandmother, my mother's mother, Elizabeth "Lizzy" Grant Reid was born in Gabarus [on April 19, 1867 and died March 16, 1944]. Her parents were Samuel Grant [1828-1909, born in St. Peters] and Ann Winnifred Woods [1831-1902, born in Gabarus]. Ann Winnifred Woods' father Thomas was born in Killarney, Ireland. She was Irish Catholic and is buried in Grand Mira. She died before I was born.

Grammy Reid was a simple hard working woman. Her home was the first off the beach. She had no maids. There was a platform at the entrance to her house that was nearest the beach. She used to scrub it with sand to keep it clean. She was always working, scrubbing the floors, taking care of the cow and chickens, cooking, knitting, making socks and mittens and taking care of my uncle who lived with them.

Grammy Reid had a cow and made butter. She raised chickens and always "set a hen" in the spring, in May. She would put a hen in a barrel with straw and 13 fertilized eggs under the hen. There was a board at the top to keep the hen inside. In three weeks, the eggs would all hatch. When we were kids we would eagerly wait for the chickens to hatch. It was a thrill.

When I was little, we needed to be completely self-sufficient. Supplies came in by boat or we grew them nearby. When I was young my Grammy Reid used to say: "March is a long hungry month…half the meat and half the hay is gone."

Grammy Reid knew how to make supplies last. She was very practical. She carried a lantern with a candle and a lamp shade over it. She would bring it over and let us blow it out. My other grandmother probably had a gaslight.

Grammy Reid was affectionate with us grandchildren. I was very close to her. She lived into my adulthood. I admired her practical skills and down-to-earth nature. My cousin Jean and I spent a lot of time with her. She took us with her picking berries and planting potatoes. When we used to jump on the ice clampers [ice floes] and we got wet, she would holler to us to stop taking such risks, but then she would lend us dry bloomers.

After Grandpa Reid died in 1939 when he was eighty, Grammy Reid always wore black. She also wore black and white aprons. They were white with little black anchors on it that her daughter-in-law Jemima made from yard goods she bought in our store. Aside from that she wore black everything, even stockings. I remember she used to buy her clothes from Eaton's catalogue.

Grammy Reid was only seventy-eight when she died in 1944, but at the time I thought she was a very old woman.

ELLA GRANT PLUNKETT
AND CAPTAIN JOHN GRANT.
CA. 1925. MILDRED GRAY
FAMILY PHOTOGRAPH.
USED WITH PERMISSION.

Grammy Grant

My other grandmother, Emma Armstrong Grant, was quite a lady and liked to have people wait on her. She had maids to do for her what my Grammy Reid did for herself. She wouldn't be seen around a hen house. My two grandmothers got along fine, although they didn't have much in common. Even though she died when I was a child, I remember Grammy Grant very well, very vividly.

Grammy Grant was descended from the earliest settlers. Her great-grandfather William Henry Bagnell [1798-1860] is listed as a native on the first census of Gabarus. He was the father of Mary Bagnell [1831-1920] who was married to Stephen Hook Armstrong. Mary and Stephen were my grandmother's parents, my great-grandparents.

Grammy Grant didn't work. She always had help. She always had everything she wanted. Grandpa Captain Grant doted on her. When Grandpa Captain Grant went to Halifax in his vessel he would bring her beautiful hats and nice clothes. Grammy Grant was very vain, always doing her hair and making sure she looked nice. They always went to church together on Sunday all dressed up.

Grammy Emma Armstrong Grant [1857-1930] was born in Gull Cove. Her father Stephen Armstrong was a mason. They had the best water well. It was very special. They always got their water there. I think there was a spring in their well, and there was also a beach by the house where they could land a small boat. The well was lined with cement, and he had a concrete foundation around his house which can still be seen today.

My great-great-grandfather William Armstrong [1805-1884] had a store in Irish Brook. His father Robert was loyal to the British crown and came to Cape Breton from the U.S. He was one of seven Armstrong men, some of whom who were loyal to the British, and some of whom settled in Kentucky.

Ancestral Family and Community

Grammy Grant always wanted to look nice. She would give us an orange if we combed her hair and rubbed her back with linament. Grandpa Grant used to say: "Put the tea on Emmy" and she would say "John, do I look presentable?" as she was puffing up her hair. And he would always say: "Yes, you look lovely", even though he wouldn't be looking at her.

Grammy Grant didn't want Wiley to marry Elsie. They thought my uncle Ernest Grant was a better match. She thought Elsie was too young, nine years younger than Wiley, but they liked her after a while. Grammy Grant had little sense of humor, especially in church. There was no fooling around. I think she was quite devout.

Grammy Grant died when I was 9, in February 1930. Shortly after that, Grandpa Captain Grant sold the house for $500 with everything in it to Harry Hardy and his wife. Harry Hardy died a few years ago, and his son sold it to Dan Wheaton. They had an auction before they sold the house, and I went to the sale. There was a big basket with a hole in the bottom that Grammy Grant used to keep oranges in at her home. It was kind of like a handbag, that size. I wanted to buy it for the memory, but someone bid against me. I couldn't go for more than $10, and someone bought it for $15.

ELSIE REID GRANT AND WILEY GRANT. 50TH WEDDING ANNIVERSARY. 1965. MILDRED GRAY FAMILY PHOTOGRAPH. USED WITH PERMISSION.

Crossing the Mira II

My mother Elsie Reid [b. 1892] and father Wiley Grant [b. 1884] knew each other since childhood. Growing up, they were almost next-door neighbors. My father was almost nine years older than my mother. He had other girlfriends, but he married Elsie in 1915 when she was 23 and he was 31. They were both good looking people who lived to celebrate their 50th wedding anniversary. But Elsie would hardly ever have her picture taken. She didn't like it. I think she was worried that she wouldn't look good.

Like my great-grandparents William and Mary Grant, my own parents had a similar mishap at the Mira River crossing in 1915 when they went into Sydney to get married.

In those days, the minister didn't come to the village that often, so people went into the city to be married. When my mother and father were married in Sydney on February 17th they went in a horse-drawn sleigh (no wheels, like Santa Claus). After the wedding, they had dinner at my Aunt Lorena's home.

Their sleigh was drawn by a horse of Grandpa Captain Grant's named Dona. He was wild. When they were on their way home a hen ran across the road at Marion Bridge and frightened Dona. The traces broke when she startled, and the horse came loose and ran away, but the sleigh kept on going toward the [Mira] river with the bride and groom. They didn't get hurt but almost went into the river and drowned. Luckily it stopped in time, and my father was able to get the horse connected to the riding sleigh again and get back on the road.

They were finally able to get home after being married and the dinner at Aunt Lorena's, and the next day they had a dance at the Intervale Hall, the building that is the community hall now. This was the first dance ever held in there. If Daddy hadn't had Ormiston in his name, he wouldn't have been able to have a dance there. I think it was kind of special to use the building. The Ormistons gave Elsie and Daddy two wicker chairs for a gift.

MILDRED GRANT AND FREDA GRANT ON PORCH OF FAMILY HOME. CA. 1923. MILDRED GRAY FAMILY PHOTOGRAPH.
USED WITH PERMISSION.

My Childhood Home

After they were married, Elsie and Wiley lived with Grammy and Grandpa Grant for a year until their house was available. Another family was living there, and my parents had to wait for them to move out. The house was built around 1912, a few years before they were married in 1915. That became my family home. At the time, the house was a lot larger. When we were growing up, there was a big kitchen and pantry in the back toward the barachois and there was a big bedroom upstairs with a walk-in closet and enough room for a youth bed in my parents' room, "my little bed." In those days there was a covered veranda at the front. In 1975, the house was renovated and the veranda was taken off.

WILEY GRANT (IN MIDDLE)
AND FRIENDS. CA. 1908.
MILDRED GRAY FAMILY
PHOTOGRAPH.
USED WITH PERMISSION.

My Father Wiley Ormiston Grant

Captain John Ormiston was a close friend of my grandfather Captain John Grant. Captain Ormiston was the captain of a two-masted schooner called the Valentine that had been built in Gabarus on Slattery Beach.

Just before what turned out to be Captain Ormiston's last voyage, Grammy Grant was expecting a baby. Captain Ormiston was going to Halifax to get a shipment of dynamite for the coal mine in Port Morien, what used to be called Cow Bay. Before he left, he stopped by and said "If it's a boy, name him after me!"

30   Bringing Out the Untold Life

On the way back, not far from Gabarus, the dynamite shifted in a storm, and the vessel blew up. The name of the boat was drifting in the ocean, the only thing left. The year was 1884. Grammy called her baby John Wiley Ormiston Grant. My father!

Daddy was a tall, muscular man with big hands, big bones. Daddy always wore a necktie and a vest even when he went out fishing. My father was a really wonderful person. He was a quiet, casual, good-natured and funny man, the kindest gentlest person. He never raised his voice or got cross. My niece Faye Libbey said that the only time she heard him yell like crazy was when she and Dennis Reid were playing in a lobster crate that fell in and floated into the bay.

Daddy was a shopkeeper, undertaker, part-time fisherman and Justice of the Peace. Uncle John Reid was also a Justice of the Peace, and they would be called in to settle disputes. Fortunately there weren't too many. They were court officials. They could make out deeds and wills and things like that.

My father was such a fine man. His death was very tough on me. Even though he was deaf, I believe that he could hear me when I said goodbye to him just before he died. Daddy had cancer, and they removed one of his legs the night he died. He died of septicemia. He didn't want to live. I prayed that he would die, so that he wouldn't be in pain.

My father never went to church except when he had to work at a funeral, but if there is a heaven my father is in it.

My Mother Elsie Reid Grant

Elsie Reid married my father Wiley Grant in 1915, and then she helped him in the store. My sister Freda was born in 1916. Elsie was 30 years old when I was born in 1920 and 43 when Ken was born. Kenneth's birth in 1932 was the first C-section done in the Sydney City Hospital in which the baby survived. The first C-section resulted in the death of both the baby and the mother. At the time I was 12 years old, and I was like a mother to Ken, since Elsie was busy in the store. I treated him like he was a doll. I loved him so much. I don't think I knew where he came from. "Family way" was whispered. I didn't know that Elsie was having a baby. At the time, she needed my help taking care of Kenneth, as she was very busy with her ice cream parlor and other things.

Just as in any family, people had different temperaments and ways of being. My mother Elsie was not affectionate. She was very busy all the time. Elsie loved her children, but couldn't show it. Although Elsie was not affectionate to her children, she was very helpful to others. She was a person of character. She was a very practical, no nonsense person. She used to say, "Cut your garment according to your cloth," make do with what you have.

Elsie was the temperamental opposite of Daddy. Elsie was dominating, very clear on standards. She showed me how to be responsible. She gave us good examples to follow. Elsie loved us, but her love was of a different kind. She wasn't a person to show emotion. Daddy was the affectionate one. He would always smile when he called me "Our Middie." My sister Freda took after Elsie. She was kind and wonderful, but not affectionate.

My parents kept good track of us to make sure we were safe. In those days, parents really looked after their children. My mother never had a babysitter, nothing like that then. Even in cities there wasn't much babysitting either. That was the way life at the time. Now it takes both parents to work to maintain a home, and people need day care. They can't usually be home with their children. Now the TV is the babysitter in a lot of families.

I don't know why, but my mother told me to call her Elsie. I called her mother until I was a mother. But when my daughter Karen was born my mother asked me to call her Elsie. Freda and Kenneth always called her Mama.

Elsie's Long Life

That word "home" is so important, so poignant "Take me home!" Home means so much. It is so tough when your elderly parents have to leave their home. They feel like life is over. My mother Elsie was in The Cove nursing home for two years before she died at ninety-six in 1988. She lived twenty-three years longer than my father. She never really had any illness, but suffered from dementia. In the end, she had a stroke at 5 p.m. and died two hours later. I hope that is the way I go too. I don't want to linger on in a nursing home.

Before my mother was in the nursing home my husband Duncan and I looked after her. Sometimes people go into a nursing home and families don't come, but we were there all the time. Kenneth used to come often, and I was there every other day. We made sure she had good clothes and good care.

In the nursing home, any nursing home, you really need someone to look after you. At that time, Elsie knew me, but she called me Annie. All the others in the nursing home were even sicker than she was. It was sad to see.

At the nursing home, they used to mix up the patients' clothes. My mother Elsie had good clothes, and we had put labels in all of them, but it still didn't help that much. When my sister Freda died when my mother was 82, it was my sister's wish that we all wear pink to her funeral. At the time I sewed my mother a pink dress. One day, I saw her pink dress on another patient at The Cove.

My Big Sister Freda

My sister Freda and I were very different. Freda was 4 years older than I. When I was 12, she was 16. That was a big age difference. We looked very different too. Freda's skin was dark and her hair coal black. She was very pretty. At the time, my hair was as white as it is now.

Freda was admired by my parents and grandparents because she was the first born and so perfect. We were friends and sisters and loved each other, but we weren't that close. I was always more relaxed than Freda. She was a perfectionist and could be very picky. She had her friends, and I had mine. And she could go to dances. When Kenneth was born, she was 16. Also, she graduated from grade 12 at age 16 and went to Sydney to school to become a nurse. Freda was very clever. She always wanted to be the best at everything. When she took her RN exam, she got the highest marks.

When she was little she lived with our parents at Grammy and Grandpa's home while my parents were waiting to take possession of our home. Freda always felt very entitled. She was always careful about appearances. Even if difficult things were going on, Freda wouldn't let on that anything was wrong. She was prideful and I think spoiled by a lot of attention when she was little. Freda had to be the head of everything. She was a perfectionist in every sense of the word. She was a head nurse for a while at the hospital in Sydney. Freda was a great person to be in charge, since she was bossy and nothing would please her unless it was perfect.

When she and Roy Libbey got married, they had the wedding at our family home. Duncan and I stood with them. Freda had three girls, Sandra, Faye, and Gail. They are very fine women. Twins are more common now than they were years ago. It was a real novelty when my sister Freda had twins, Sandra and Gail. They weighed 5 and 6 pounds and were totally healthy. They weren't identical, but Freda kept the kids dressed the same until they were 9 years old. Faye was born 12 years after Sandra and Gail.

LEFT TO RIGHT
FREDA GRANT, MILDRED GRANT, JEAN REID. MILDRED GRAY FAMILY PHOTOGRAPH. USED WITH PERMISSION.

Freda always wanted to put her best foot forward. She would spend two weeks cleaning her house for the bridge club. She used a Q-tip to clean in corners. The day her husband Roy Libbey died suddenly of a heart attack in 1966, she was fifty-three years old. Shortly after, she sold the house, moved to Ontario from Sydney, bought a car and took driving lessons. Freda worked as a registered nurse in a nursing home in London, Ontario.

After Roy's death, I helped her raise the three girls, and we are still very close, like my own daughters. Freda died in surgery at sixty-two having a heart operation in Montreal. After she died they saw that her heart was in really bad shape, that she had a congenital heart disease. At the time, my mother was eighty-two, and it was an awful thing for her. My mother never really got over it. Freda was her favorite. It was my sister's wish that we all wear pink to her funeral, and we did.

I was the opposite of Freda. She was perfect and never got into trouble. I was the one who got in trouble, more like harmless mischief and pranks than real trouble, no one hurting anyone. I was the middle child and made do with hand-me-downs. Freda wouldn't let me touch her dolls or her doll carriage. But she was a good woman, and I looked up to her goodness as a role model. I appreciated her. Freda was a wonderful person. She read the Bible through and through.

Ancestral Family and Community   35

Grandpa Grant adored her. Freda was always first. When I was a teenager, she wasn't around that much. If she was home she was studying, since she was not an outdoor person. I would be out in a snow bank, and she was in the house. I was more adventurous. I am still more adventurous than most.

When I was a child, I was always active, swimming, skating and running around. I did a lot of baking and cooking but not cleaning. I was a poor candidate for housework. I didn't know anything about housekeeping. Someone else did it. Freda's job was cleaning on Saturday. I remember that Freda would clean lampshades.

I was outdoors all the time. I was probably hauling my traps out in the barachois or rowing a boat. I probably would have been considered a tom-boy.

Freda was like Aunt Ella. She always wore matching clothes. She was so perfect. Was she happy? I don't think she could have been.

The Boston States

Around the turn of the century a lot of people wanted to go to Boston to live and work. At that time, Boston was the main place we heard about, the "Boston States" with Cape Bretoners going there as domestics for well-off families. In a couple of cases I know, the girls married the sons of the families for whom they worked in Massachusetts. Domestics would get connected by word-of-mouth and letter. That was the basic communication at the turn of the century. That was also a time when a lot of people left small villages like Gabarus to find work elsewhere. People who went would pave the way for others, telling them about opportunities. They would get the train from Sydney and go across the Strait of Canso in a train ferry.

My Aunt Ella went to Boston in 1902 when she was 23 years old. Ella went with her cousin Margaret MacDonald (my husband Duncan's mother's sister). It was very easy to immigrate then, and if you married an American you were automatically an American. You didn't need a green card or need to be sponsored. You just went ahead and got a job. Margaret went to work in a store, and Ella went to work for a milliner, the same kind of work she had done in Sydney. Aunt Ella probably couldn't have been a domestic. She was never any good at housekeeping.

When the owner of that millinery shop died, his wife decided to sell the business to Ella, and Ella became a successful businesswoman. Her third floor millinery shop was in a nice building on Boylston Street, right next door to Jordan Marsh. "Margaret Eleanor Grant, Owner" was painted on the glass entry door. Aunt Ella made and decorated hats with flowers and feathers.

When she first went to Boston she boarded for some time in Cambridge with Annie Stacey, another cousin from Gabarus. Other young people used to come to their home for musical gatherings with piano playing and singing. That is how Aunt Ella met her future husband-- Albert "Bert" Plunkett, an Irish Catholic American who was already successful at Raymond and Whitcomb Cruise Lines at a time when steamship travel around the world was coming into vogue. Annie knew him and invited him on a night when there were a lot of young people, including Ella.

Bert was upper class and well educated. And Ella was bright and interested in everything. Elsie used to say "Ella was so stylish!" Ella was funny, had a good sense of humor, very charming. Ella and Bert went together for three or four years before they married. He was away a lot on trips.

In 1915, Aunt Ella and Uncle Bert were married in the Grand Mira Catholic Church which was fancier than the Gabarus Catholic Church. In those days intermarriage was a really big deal, and sometimes it made a rift in a family that never healed. When Aunt Ella got married her mother Grammy Grant made her a traditional marriage quilt, but didn't give it to her then, or ever. I have the quilt. Ella knew that her parents didn't approve of her marrying a Catholic, but she didn't care. She wanted to marry him. Grammy Grant refused to come to the wedding. His family didn't approve of his marrying a Protestant. Bert had a sister who was an organist in the Catholic Church in Newton [Massachusetts] for 40 years, but I didn't really know her.

When Aunt Ella married Uncle Bert she automatically became an American. After Ella got married and was traveling she closed her business. That kind of business was going out of style anyway.

After a while, Grammy Grant started to appreciate Bert. Later, when they came home to visit it was a special event. When Ella and Bert came, it was like the king and queen visiting. When I was a little girl I remember Ella and Bert visiting Gabarus every other summer. When I was growing up, people went from Gabarus to Boston to visit their families. Usually people didn't come from Boston to Gabarus.

Grammy Grant would get a lady to make donuts when Ella visited, and Aunt Ella and Uncle Bert used to bring watermelon when they came. It was the first one I had ever seen. All of us kids had to be dressed up for the visit, and she used to bring my sister Freda and me dresses from Boston too.

I remember when I was 5 years old. This would have been 1925. I remember wearing a hat that was a bit torn and Aunt Ella said, "You wouldn't think Elsie would put a hat on a child with its brim torn!" But I piped up: "I am not wearing my Sunday hat on a weekday!!" I stuck up for myself.

From that time on, Aunt Ella played a big role in my life. She expanded my world. Aunt Ella read a lot, studied languages, and traveled all over the world. Ella enlarged my perspective. Ella helped me. I would never have been able to travel. I was 16 before I even saw Halifax. She gave me that opportunity.

Aunt Ella and Uncle Bert lived on 11 Vineyard Rd. in Newton Center from 1929 to 1965 or so. They had a beautiful rose garden in the back. I started to look after them in 1947 when Ella was sixty-eight. I went there twice a year for two to three weeks each time, every spring and every fall. I did this for just over thirty years, until she died at the age of ninety-eight. She paid my way and gave me money when I was there. When I was away, I organized workers to do the telegraph or the switchboard.

My Aunt Ella was a very vain beautiful woman with lovely black hair. I believe that pride prevented her from wanting children. But she was always generous to me. Aunt Ella used to tell me: "When I die you can see the world." At the time, I thought that Boston was the end of the world.

My mother thought Ella was too stylish and no good at housework. In that era, there was a distinct class system, and Ella wanted to be friends with notable, well educated people. Aunt Ella always had a maid, a black woman named Ada from the West Indies who lived in the attic of her home. Like all rich people Aunt Ella had a set of rules that Ada had to follow. She had a weekly massage on a Tuesday from her private masseuse. I tried to get there then, so I could get a massage too! This was when I was in my fifties.

Uncle Bert was an angel, a wonderful man, so good natured, cheerful and generous too. Aunt Ella kept diaries, and I have some of them still. In her diary from one trip she wrote "Bert said how beautiful I looked, yet I had gained 25 pounds since I started traveling." Bert always said nice things to me too. He used to exclaim: "I like the way you cook bacon, Mildred!" Meaning that I didn't burn it?!

Bert was so loving to her, always telling her how nice she looked. Very devoted. He was so good to me too. We used to laugh a lot. Bert loved little kids, but Ella didn't want children.

UNCLE BERT PLUNKETT AND AUNT ELLA GRANT PLUNKETT CA. 1929. MILDRED GRAY FAMILY PHOTOGRAPH. USED WITH PERMISSION.

She said she never did anything to prevent getting pregnant, but I don't believe she wanted any.

Ella and Bert had a blue Persian cat named Maggie. She was so smart. She knew Uncle Bert's car, and when she heard it she would get up off the windowsill and go to the door to meet Bert.

We always went to Cape Cod for a week in early summer to their house there. We were always there for my birthday on May 13th, staying in a house across the street from the Kennedy compound in Hyannis.

Aunt Ella's cousin Margaret, with whom she went to Boston, was the mother of Donald Ross, an editor of the Boston Herald. I saw him when I went to Boston. When he retired he lived on Cape Cod. Ella and Margaret were first cousins. My great-grandmother Mary was a MacDonald, and her brother Joe was Duncan's grandfather (his mother's father).

Ella's friends were like her, rich women with maids. Polly Hood was one of my Aunt Ella's good friends. Polly went to Boston from North Sydney to be a domestic to work in the home of a rich family, the Hoods. They had a big dairy business.

MILDRED GRAY IN BOSTON, CA. 1950S. MILDRED GRAY FAMILY PHOTOGRAPH. USED WITH PERMISSION.

The wife was sick, and she died. Later, Mr. Hood fell in love with Polly, and they were married. Many attractive young women from Cape Breton fell in love with their bosses in Boston.

Lou and Marjorie were two other good friends. They would come over about once a week for afternoon tea. They would have teas too, and she would go to their house. Some of them would travel with her. Aunt Ella would tinkle the bell, and Ada would come. Ella liked keeping up with the Joneses. She really enjoyed her upper class status.

I played a role in that circle of women. I did sewing then. I made all my own clothes. I used to take up their hems and help them out a little with sewing and alterations. I made dresses for Aunt Ella. There was one in particular with a jacket that I made that she really liked. Most of the time, she used to buy her dresses on the 3rd floor of Jordan Marsh.

Aunt Ella was always asking me to do simple things in the home. I used to bake for them. Uncle Bert used to say "Here comes Mildred! Let's get the flour out! Bert was a good cook too, and he liked to cook, but she wouldn't let him. The maid did the cooking most of the time.

Ancestral Family and Community

When I was at her home in Newton Center, I saw how other people lived, what they ate, how they dressed, and what they talked about. Aunt Ella was a reader and took courses in languages. She was fluent in French by taking private lessons and teaching herself. Bert was always reading too, and he could speak four languages. As a world traveler, he actually knew a few words in almost every language. Aunt Ella and Uncle Bert had season's tickets to the opera, and I learned to love opera too.

In many ways, Ella was generous to me, but she was the vainest person in the world. At Jordan Marsh they sold a mirror with lights on the side, 2-3 bulbs on each side. Aunt Ella asked me to go and get it. It was raining, and I had to take a bunch of buses. When I finally got back to the house and unpacked it and turned it on, she said, "I don't have that many wrinkles! This mirror is not right! Take it right back!" She was 85 at the time. Ella said: "I never had a wrinkle until I looked in that mirror!"

Aunt Ella was generous to other people too. There was a charcoal picture of Joan of Arc on the wall of her house; her doctor admired it, and she gave it to him. There was one of Mount Fuji that her lawyer admired, and she gave it to him.

When I was looking after my Aunt Ella, she almost kept the drugstore open buying all kinds of cosmetics. She was never sick. It was down the street from where she lived. So I used to see the druggist quite a bit. He didn't know much about Canada. I would be there in May, and the druggist would say: "Are you still skiing up north?" And he always asked about the Mounties in red uniforms walking around the streets. That was his image of Canada, from the movies. We knew more about the U.S. than people knew about Canada. I think that is still true, although I'll bet that half of the people in Massachusetts came from Canada at one time. In my day, if you married an American you were automatically an American. When the war was on, a lot of people signed up for the military. So many families had roots in Canada. But some were not Americans until the war. When they enlisted in the war, they made a choice to be one or the other. They had to pledge allegiance to the U.S. and give up their Canadian citizenship. Now you can have dual citizenship.

When I was away from home taking care of Aunt Ella, my daughter Karen went with my mother Elsie, and Albert would stay home with Duncan. Nancy would go to her Aunt Edith Hardy on Duncan's side (to the home on Seaview where she lives now). Nancy even looks like Edith. For the Morse Office they would send a woman to cover when I was away. When I ran the switchboard I would organize coverage when I was with Aunt Ella. When I wasn't home Duncan cooked all the meals. He cooked steak, simple food. Duncan never wanted to travel. When I went to Boston, I would be gone for two or three weeks at a time. Then later when I took the eight trips Ella gave me, I was away then too, although the kids were out of the house by then.

I didn't ever want the kind of life Aunt Ella had with someone waiting on me. I wouldn't like to tinkle the bell. I like to have what I need, but I never envied luxury. It is nice to see it though. Even then, their clothes were different. When I started to go to Boston, rich people had one type of clothes and poor people another.

But I wanted to travel, learn, and see how others lived, especially compared to when I was there before. Times change. It is good to see it and to learn.

Ella gave me money for helping her. She paid my way and gave me spending money. I would take the bus to Boston on Mackenzie Bus Lines, traveling all day and all night. We stopped at the border and showed our identification, but there were few restrictions then. I would have a lot of things coming back. Even bedding was different in Boston, better quality, especially cotton. I always bought the kids things. I used to get clothes in Filene's basement to bring them. In those days nice shoes in Filene's basement cost a dollar a pair. I remember buying jumper dresses from the bins for my girls. In Gabarus, they were the best dressed in school.

Aunt Ella maintained journals when she travelled. I have one journal from a cruise to the Holy Land. I have one when she was a big woman, very overweight, but she entered a beauty contest, and she won, even though she had gained 20 pounds since she left home. Bert liked her fat, and he was fat too.

MILDRED GRAY WORLD TRAVELER. CA. 1978. MILDRED GRAY FAMILY PHOTOGRAPH. USED WITH PERMISSION.

Bert had Parkinson's for 24 years and had to retire early as VP of Raymond Whitcomb Cruise Lines. Uncle Bert died when he was in his late 70s. Although Bert was Catholic, Aunt Ella buried him in a Protestant cemetery. Aunt Ella is buried next to him.

After Bert died, I helped Aunt Ella sell their home and move into an apartment on Hunnewell Avenue in Newton. It was a big apartment but a lot smaller than her house. She had a living room and a kitchenette and a bedroom and bathroom.

Aunt Ella was ninety-eight years old when she died in 1976. She didn't want to live to be a hundred. That wasn't the style. But she outlived my father who died in 1965. I was fifty-six years old when she died, and I had been helping her since I was in my twenties. In the end, she died from a kidney infection, anemia and old age. She had been in the hospital for three weeks. She once weighed 220 pounds. When she died, she weighed less than 100 pounds.

The week before Aunt Ella died I went to Boston. At the time, she was in the hospital. When I went to visit her, she said "In the presence of my lawyer I want to give my diamond rings and watch to my niece Mildred. The one who gave them to me loved me, and I dearly love her." After I left and had just arrived back in Gabarus I heard that she died, on Halloween night. I flew right back to Boston and stayed at the Howard Johnson's in Newton.

Aunt Ella's lawyer in Boston handled the estate and her bequests. I served as executor of her estate. She used to say: "My niece Mildred never saw anything of the world," and she wanted to do something about it. Thanks to Aunt Ella, I traveled to Paris and many other fascinating and faraway places after she died and willed me eight trips abroad, all expenses paid. For me, the memories were more important than the money. Now people travel everywhere, and it is helping to bring the world closer together.

MILDRED GRAY, SALMON
FISHING IN KOMOX, B.C.
CA. 1988. MILDRED GRAY
FAMILY PHOTOGRAPH.
USED WITH PERMISSION.

I always traveled alone, because Duncan didn't like to travel. My first trip was to London, and I stayed at the Imperial Hotel, and I went on a bus tour. Later I went to France, Germany, Italy, Switzerland, and Bermuda. I used a credit card that the lawyer gave me.

I also went to Houston to see my cousin Neil Armstrong's uniform that he wore on the moon walk. My grandmother was an Armstrong, and Neil Armstrong was a distant cousin. The Armstrong family originally came from Scotland. We were descended from a family of seven Armstrong brothers. Around the time of the American Revolution some stayed in Kentucky, and some came north. I was from the one who was loyal to the British, and American astronaut Neil Armstrong was the great-great-grandson of one of the ones who stayed in Kentucky. When I was in Australia on a trip, I coincidentally met a man named John Armstrong. He was the one who told me all about the Armstrongs, since he and his sister were doing genealogy research. Later he came to Gabarus for two visits.

I also traveled to California, South Carolina, and Arizona. I have been to more than twenty-five of the fifty states and every province in Canada. One of my desires in life was to be able to walk in each province in Canada which happily, and luckily, I was able to do, also many states in the U.S. and other countries.

Aunt Ella's friend Marjorie Erskine gave me a bequest of $1,000 when she died. With the exchange rate at the time, the family sent me $750. Marjorie owned a lot of land near Aunt Ella's. She owned a house where there is now a shopping center. She died after Aunt Ella.

There was no doubt about what I had to do for Ella's funeral. Aunt Ella liked to control things. At least one year before she died, we had gone together to the undertaker to pick out the clothes that she would wear at the funeral parlor. She wanted to wear an Alice blue robe and jewelry and glasses. She always wore glasses.

Aunt Ella had written it all down, who she wanted at the funeral and who she wanted to perform the service. Aunt Ella didn't go to church, but there was a minister she wanted at her funeral, a retired minister who had been Polly Hood's minister from North Sydney. She had a list of eight people she wanted at her funeral, but only one was alive when she died.

There were seven guests at the funeral. The seven people at Aunt Ella's funeral were the lawyer and his wife, me, Aggie, a cousin of mine, and a friend of Aunt Ella's, Marjorie Erskine, and another two women, old friends.

Before the service I lifted up the corner of the casket to make sure she had the dress and the beads she wanted. She did. The service was in the chapel of the funeral home, and then we went to the cemetery and had a short graveside service. She wasn't very religious. That is what she wanted. It was all arranged.

Although it was only November 2, it was blowing a gale of wind and it was snowing at the cemetery. I had never been in a limousine. I was amazed that there was a phone. It was a very short service. We sang a hymn I picked out, "Softly and Tenderly Jesus is Calling, *calling for you and for me…..Come home, come home, ye who are weary, come home.*"

I can always find Uncle Bert's and Aunt Ella's graves in the Newton cemetery, "Ella M. Plunkett," since it is right next to Polly Hood's big monument on which is chiseled: "Love joins our present with the past and the future" by Kahlil Gibran.

MEMORIES OF THE LAST CENTURY IN GABARUS FROM HORSE-DRAWN SLEIGH TO INTERNET

Captain John Grant in the Era of Sail

In my grandfather's time, at the end of the 19th century, there were educated captains and self-educated ship's captains. My father's close friend Captain John Ormiston had captain's papers, and my grandfather had formal papers too. Now I think that you have to have papers, no matter who owns the boat, even if it is your own. Captains have to take a course and pass a test now. But in my grandfather's time, if you had a two-masted sailing ship, some charts and a sextant, you could undertake a shipping business. They were skilled in navigating by the stars. I think the vessels also sailed close to the Atlantic Coast. If you had your own vessel, you were automatically a captain of your ship. They were courageous, but they didn't know they were. That is just what they did.

Until 1902, when he sold his last vessel, my grandfather Captain John Grant used his sailing vessels to transport supplies to stores, including ours. His vessels were entirely sail powered. He was an excellent sailor, completely self-taught. At that time, a lot of people had their own vessels, they were building them here in Gabarus. There was a family of shipbuilders in nearby Fourchu too, the Hoopers.

Becoming a ship captain was a good way to make a living for enterprising men who didn't want to become fishermen. Many had two-masted vessels built and went to sea. Grandpa Captain Grant was doing the route from Cape Breton to Halifax and Boston carrying supplies back and forth. Grandpa Grant bought the three ships he owned. He owned them one at a time. He was able to find all the crew from here, and my father went with him too. It was common for the captain to have his son as first mate. When he sold his last vessel he went into business with his father. At that time Gabarus was a thriving town. After my grandfather gave up the sea, they started to have gas engines.

For well over 100 years, two-masted vessels, many of which were built in Gabarus, would go to Barbados with barrels of mackerel and sometimes timber and coal. In 1915 the tourist business in steam ships started. Even into the 1960s, although it was steamers then, not schooners, mackerel was shipped to Barbados.

When the fish arrived in Barbados they used to dry and smoke it. The fish was packed in reused puncheons or wood barrels that were large, about 45 gallons or more. A lot of the barrels were made in Chester, near Halifax, and shipped to Gabarus on boats.

Grandpa Captain Grant's three ships were the Minnie, the Hector MacGregor and the Pluma. I think the Hector MacGregor was his last ship, and he sold the vessel to John Grant in Port Hawkesbury. He was no relation to us, but later my grandfather visited him and saw the boat where it had been put ashore. The Hector MacGregor ship name also became a person's name. One granddaughter of Captain Grant had a baby and wanted a girl but had a boy. "What shall we call him?" "Call him Hector MacGregor." He is now a Toronto lawyer, named after a boat!

Ship Building

At the turn of the century in Gabarus, in the inlet of the Upper Barachois, they used to build ships on the beach. I know of several. There were lots of vessels out of Gabarus and lots of ship's captains. Two-masted schooners are what they built here. Ships were built in Gabarus where the [Methodist] church used to be, in the inlet, across from where the pink house is now. Robert Noble built a two-masted ship on Margaret Grant's field, three houses up from the beach.

Isaiah MacDonald, another captain from Gabarus, had captain's papers and so did my cousin Charlie Reid, my grandfather Albert Reid's brother. Charlie Reid was the master of a four-masted schooner in New York harbour, but they eliminated four-masted schooners because it was too heavy for the size of the ship. After he came home from New York, he started fishing. Shipbuilders could build anything, houses, and churches. Dan Harris' grandfather was a sea captain, and he built my daughter Nancy's house. Later, he moved to Louisbourg.

Gull Cove

Gull Cove was once a thriving community. There was once a road to Gull Cove across the beach, a road down around Ram's Head. Then a lot of people moved to Gabarus, "The Harbour", where they used to come for groceries.

Now that road is eroded. It went by Ram's Head, then Harris Lake. There were two roads going to Gull Cove. Most recently, with the erosion on the shore road that we used to call "the grassy road," people go down Gull Cove Road by the [Lakeview] cemetery. The first car that went to Gull Cove probably around the early twenties belonged to my friend's father. He went on the road by the cemetery. Lowell Point was another place where people lived. There was a woman at the Cape [Gabarus], past Gull Cove, about five miles from Gabarus. Everyone used to go down there, walking or on ATVs for picnics and berry picking, but it is almost impassable now, part of the protected Gabarus Wilderness.

Turn of the Century

A lot of people moved to town [Sydney] when the steel plant opened in 1902. Fishing was poor at the time. Fish was selling for 2 cents, and lobster was 3 cents a pound. Along our rocky coastline, fishermen used rowboats to do their fishing. It is really hard work. Better paying, and easier jobs could be had in Sydney.

Some people commuted at first, but many moved to Sydney. In those days, you could commute by ferryboat to and from Louisbourg every morning. You could get the train there to take you to Sydney and back. People would go to Sydney by car too.

The early explorers to Cape Breton used to say that codfish were so dense and plentiful that you could almost walk on water. In my day cod fishing brought in much more money than lobster. Lobster brought in 2-3 cents a pound when I was a child. The price went up to fifty-three cents a pound on the last week of the season when we bought lobster around the 80s. This area is now closed to cod fishing, but in two years it is supposed to come back. In my day, cod fishing was very big, now it is lobster and crabs. It has been only fifteen years for crabs.

When I was a teenager in the 1930s, a lobster license was 25 cents. When my friend Margaret and I were about 13-14 years old, we went into the lobster business. We paid the 25 cents for a license, and we had ten lobster traps. Grandpa Captain Grant helped us, especially with pulling up the traps. Grandpa had a rowboat with a sail that Grammy made out of 100-pound flour sacks. We had our lobster traps right by this side of Rouse Island near the beach. There is a rock out there, Carline Rock, and that is where we set our traps, by the gut rocks.

The boat would lean from one side to another according to the way the wind was. I was afraid, but Margaret wasn't. We called the trap that caught the most a "flapjack," because it needed a lot of repair. We would sell the lobsters we caught to a man out by the gut rock, the entrance into the barachois. He had a "smack," a big boat with an open deck, probably 38 feet long.

The boat was anchored there, and then he would put them in lobster crates in the water, and, at the end of the day, he would take them in his boat to the factory at "The Level," the area between the Bay and the Upper Barachois. At the time he was the only buyer. In those days, lobster was 5 cents a pound, and sometimes we would get a couple a day. One day I remember we caught two lobsters, one little one and one big one. We made 15-20 cents, and Margaret and I split it. We didn't catch many, but it was fun. At the end of the season, we each had five dollars. We thought we were rich. Later on our summer trip to Sydney we had money to buy something for ourselves.

A lot of kids had licenses when I was a kid. In those days you only had to have a license for lobster. It has all changed. I think now it costs $150,000 for a license, and you can't get a license unless you are in the commercial fishing business. You didn't need a license for codfish. Now you have to have a license for almost every kind of fish, lobsters, scallops, crabs. You don't need a license to jig mackerel, and you don't need a license for capelin. Some people still sell capelin to the boats for bait.

Old Fashioned Values

The Gabarus community was very close. We had good education, lots of recreation and very supportive family and friends around us. When I grew up there was no discrimination. No one cared if you were rich or poor. People were good to each other. People are natural here, educated people and their children, a lot of accomplished people, quiet, loving, caring. Everyone looked after each other. Everyone knew everyone, and everyone depended on each other. It was the simple life. That is what we knew.

In Gabarus, time stands still. All the old fashioned values still live here: human friendship, caring people, everyone accepting everyone. People share what they have. People are flexible and giving. If you need anything you can get it from your neighbors, tools, any kind of support. There are people who are financially rich, but they may not have what we had. Everyone here helps each other. That is how it is yet.

I learned a lot of lessons from what I have seen in my nine decades. I learned from my work and the way I had to do things. I like to learn something every day. I was connected to a lot of young people. I like people. I like company. I believe that resilient is the way you should be if you are not dead.

1920s Gabarus

GABARUS. RED CROSS CARAVAN, 6 AUGUST 1920; NSA, HELEN CREIGHTON FONDS, ALBUM 12 NO. 68

When I was a little girl in the 1920s, Gabarus was a lively community of about 500 people. We had seven stores, a doctor and a dentist. The land was more open than it is now, less forested. We were more open to the lake and the ocean. It seems that in the last ten years, the trees just grew up like crazy. When I was growing up, I never saw finches like I do now. In my day, there were sparrows and robins in the spring, quite a few robins.

When I was growing up in the 1920s and 30s everyone had a barn, and most everyone had a cow and a pig. Not many people had horses, even in my time. People had fences around their property then. They were open fences but high enough to keep the animals in, about four feet high. The odd person had a horse until 1945, but there were cows into the 60s, mostly used for cow's milk for their family. People didn't sell their milk. They used it for their own family. In nearby Grand Mira the farmers sold their milk, butter, and produce. There are farms there still. From those farms we got potatoes, turnips and carrots for the store. We traded for tea and molasses, all kinds of groceries.

I dream every night, mostly about my childhood, things that I did when I was a child. I dream about Grammy Reid who had a cow and the barn. We had milk from her cow. We never had pasteurization, so the milk always tasted great. As long as the cow was healthy, and the cows were healthy, there was no need for pasteurization. Grammy Reid made butter that tasted so good. Grammy's butter was not as yellow as some people's, but I loved her butter. We had the store too, and we always sold creamy butter.

Jim and Dan MacDonald might have been the last to have cows, probably up to 1965. Up until then, it was kind of a necessity. People needed cream and milk. The cows ate the grass. The MacDonalds lived next door to the store, and they had a separator for cream.

When Grammy Reid had a cow, long before they had a separator, she had a basin, a shallow bowl. She would pour the milk into the basin about 6 inches high.

Overnight, the cream would rise and she would skim that off and make butter. They couldn't refrigerate the milk. They would put their milk in a small covered bucket and lower it into the well 10-15 feet deep to keep it cool.   Right over by my apple tree, the well was 13 feet deep. In those days, wells were open with a wooden cover.

There has always been enough water here. Remember that people didn't use water then like they do now. People used water more carefully. Sponge baths to conserve water. Once a week. We didn't have time to spend a lot of time taking baths and showers. People needed water for their cows, unless you lived on a stream. All the wells were dug wells. In 1947, the old well at my home was blocked, we had a man light a dynamite stick, and it opened up the rock bottom and the water sprang up like a geyser.

When I was little I was bathed in the wash tub in the kitchen. In my day everyone had two pair of bloomers. We would change underwear and bathe on Saturday. Then we would change clothes for Sunday. Every day we would clean our teeth.

Monday was washday. Before electricity it was hard to do the wash. Most people had a wash tub and a scrubbing board. They would heat water in pots. We were a little better off than some. When I was little, we had a washer with a wooden tub with a plunger that you had to pull by hand after you put the clothes in the water. But most washed their clothes by hand. We all had to put clothes on the line, even in winter. There was a gas washer at my mother-in-law's home. You had to fill it with water by the pot full. For dinner on Monday washday we always had scrunchions: codfish and fried pork rinds.

People worked hard. It was a way of life. We didn't know any different. Most people didn't travel far from home. Few people had cars, very few, including my family. At the time, most business was conducted in Louisbourg. Many times, I rode my bike to Louisbourg. Along the old road, it is about twelve miles direct. There was also the ferry from Gabarus to Louisbourg until the 1940s after the war. From there you could take a train to Sydney or Glace Bay. It was called the Sydney and Louisbourg Railroad, and they had a Morse Code key on the train.

In winter, using a horse and sleigh was the only way to get into Gabarus, since the ferry boat didn't run in the winter.

Pound Party

People here have always helped each other, since the beginning of the community. In the old days, people would have a "pound party." Everyone who went brought a pound of something like tea, sugar, flour, or soap. People used to bring a fiddle or a mouth organ and sometimes have a dance. I remember hearing about a pound party at Daddy's Aunt Sarah in Gull Cove. Daddy told me that she had a cat with one eye, and she charged money to see her cat.

Down and Out in Gabarus

Aunt Ella and Uncle Bert lost a lot of money in the Depression. But here in Gabarus the Depression wasn't an issue. We were doing the same thing. At that time, some people came from Sydney to try to get into the fishing business. They just needed to work, whether they had any ability or not. Someone might ask: "Did you know there was a tramp into the village? I wonder where he will stay tonight." He might stay all winter and help around the place. Gabarus people were accepting. That is the type of people who are still here. Very little prejudice. People would put him to work, help them as much as they could. A lot of them got work with the fishermen. Mostly this was during the Depression, people "from away" who were down and out.

Healthy Eating and Hard Work

I have been healthy my whole life. Most people were quite healthy. All our food was organic, no insecticides, no fertilizer, no preservatives. People were not overweight. Also people were outdoors a lot, and that helps. Too much sun is bad for their skin, but only recently did we know about the danger of skin cancer from a lot of outdoor activities without sunscreen. Sunscreen was unheard of when I was growing up.

I think in some cases people were healthier then. Meat was not cured. I think people ate more natural, more organic. I ate all the fat off of everything when I was little, and at my age I have virtually no heart disease. There was no such thing as hot dogs. We ate corned beef, turnip, potatoes, cabbage, and carrots. My Aunt Jemima had a garden and grew lettuce at her home on Gull Cove Road. We used to eat that with vinegar and sugar. We would pick carrots out of the ground, rub them on the grass and eat them. Any food in moderation is fine. My Great Grammy Grant lived to be more than a hundred. She ate everything. She had to eat what she could. She had no choice. But she had also worked hard at all the chores.

In my time, a few people, only five or six families, had kitchen gardens with some flowers and potatoes, carrots, turnips. Most everyone ate a lot of fish. We ate codfish and mackerel and fish cakes. Daddy didn't like herring. He liked salted dried codfish with pork scraps. That is called "scrunchions" in Newfoundland, what we always had for Monday washday.

In my day no one had time to get sick. People worked all summer, fall, winter and spring. Taking care of the cow and other animals, cooking, canning, sewing, making mats, taking care of gardens, drying fish, so much to do all year long.

Everyone worked hard. Elias Sherwood would butcher his pig in November, and I think he helped others too, since he knew how to do it. I remember that he was a hardworking man. His father was from England. He was married here, and he had 12-14 children. Unfortunately, many died in childhood.

Breakfast, Lunch, and Pies

For breakfast in our home the children would have porridge or corn flakes or eggs and toast. Elsie made her own bread. We had dinner at noon of vegetables and meat. Then supper was 5 p.m. when we would have bacon, potatoes, hash and eggs. Those were our big meals of the day, and we all sat around the table. There was no taking your plate here and there. We talked about the store and things that were happening. I remember that my father liked barley soup for supper.

My mother baked pies on Saturday, and we didn't think it was hard. On Saturdays all the women in the village made pies. In those days, people would buy 100 pound bags of flour for the winter. In my day, I never saw a package of flour. Everyone would make at least five pies on Saturday, mostly apple, from dried apples cut in rounds. There were lots of great apple trees in Gabarus. I remember the smell of the pies baking in the oven. That smell still evokes a wonderful feeling.

In summer, the type of pies followed the berries as they came. In July, we picked bakeapple berries; at the end of July, it was blueberries; and in the fall, it was foxberries and cranberries. In my day, everyone went to Grant's Barren across from Lakeview Cemetery to pick very small red bakeapples, foxberries or cranberries. You would walk a mile on Grant's Barrens. I picked white lilies out of the lily pond on the barren. There is nothing like the beautiful smell of lilies. We would lay them on top of the berries. We always had cream, since everyone had a cow. With fresh cream and lots of sugar there was nothing more delicious.

There is also a great berry picking place at a heritage cemetery in Framboise. To get there from Gabarus you turn left at the cairn on Crooked Lake Road in Framboise and follow that road. The old cemetery is on the ocean. A lot of Scottish people came there.

In our family we always had something sweet after dinner, like apple pie. My dad loved sweets, and he would add sugar to the pie. They would be sweet, but he would always add more sugar. We had apple pie with cream. Elsie made gingersnaps, and I used to dip them in milk, and I thought they were wonderful. After I grew up I didn't like milk. Now I haven't had milk for more than 70 years.

Barter for Butter

Everybody ate better from the country then. In Grand Mira (we called that the "country," Marion Bridge too) they would sell their butter to our store in a patty, like a fish cake, wrapped in a rhubarb leaf and a little wooden peg to hold it firm. Now I read that rhubarb leaf is poison. We didn't eat the leaf, but it kept it clean and cool. That was their refrigeration. From Grand Mira, they would bring out 10 pounds of butter at a time in a big round stoneware jug to hold it.

The farmers would buy tea and sugar and flour, and my grandfather and father would barter with them, giving them supplies in exchange for butter. It was the same with fish. They might use fish as a currency to pay for other things they wanted. I am actually not crazy about fish. We had it in the store, but we didn't eat a lot of fish when I was growing up. At that time, it was only a cent a pound. T-bone steak or rib roast is my favorite, preferably from the western part of Canada.

In Grand Mira last Saturday I saw a ninety year old man. I remembered him at the age of ten when he would bring little buckets full of wild strawberries to Grant's store. I told him about it, and he remembered. In those days, he charged 25 cents a bucket for the strawberries.

Hooking Mats

My mother couldn't sew or knit, but she made hooked mats that she would barter for Congoleum. This was about the time I was 5 years old. In the winter, women would hook mats, and in the spring a man came around with oil cloth rugs, Congoleum, about 9 x 9 feet square. He would take hand-hooked mats in exchange. My mother got a couple of Congoleum squares, in exchange for big hooked mats.

I had an older aunt, Mary Armstrong in Gull Cove, who made Sunday mats and everyday mats. They did their own designs in those days. After a while there were stamped mats where you followed the colors. Some people would draw flowers on the burlap and hook it in a wooden frame.

If you had leftover rags you would make a mat called a "bunch mat" of wider strips, softer, any leftover material. You hooked with what you had. Some ladies made beautiful mats. Women in the village still make mats. They have a class every week.

At that time, there were not a lot of people who sewed in the village. Duncan's mother Elizabeth Gray sewed, crocheted, knitted, everything. Sometimes people would make their own yarn. My mother Elsie couldn't sew a stitch. It was Duncan's mother who taught me to sew. She was very capable. She did a lot of sewing, for herself and other people. She made Aunt Jemima's wedding dress. She was a very good at it, and I watched her and learned. She had a Singer sewing machine. Everyone had Singers. It was a treadle machine. Sewing? I learned by doing. "Necessity is the mother of invention." In this life we learn by example, by watching other people. Later, my sewing came in handy as a way to make extra money when I visited Aunt Ella, and I used to make and sell quilts too.

Pre-electric World

In the pre-electric world it was a very different feeling, a different lifestyle. Our senses were different. At the time, people used wood or coal burning stoves to heat their home. I miss the smell of spruce burning in the fireplaces of neighboring homes. In the store we had a potbellied stove in the middle of the floor. We burned coal there and also at home in the kitchen stove. We had a stove in the living room and a stove upstairs too. There was also a pipe from downstairs that heated the upstairs. It was always warm in our home. I remember that feeling of warmth and security. We always had a hot water tank on the stove. When I was little, I used to bathe in the bathtub by the stove. We had to haul our own water, but it was routine. We were used to it. Women especially worked so hard. After electricity, we were in another world, easier. To go from no electricity to electricity was a huge shift.

Before 1947, there were no streetlights in Gabarus. At Grandpa Grant's store there were gas lights, and one in each home in the village. That was in the 1930s. Before that it was kerosene oil. The hanging lamps in the church were kerosene. At the time, most people didn't have flashlights, but Grandpa sold flashlights in the store and later gas lamps, but we had to be very careful with any light.

A few people used gas irons for ironing clothes. There was a place on the back that you put propane gas in the back and you pumped it up and lit it with a match. Otherwise you would heat the iron on the stove. Elsie had a gas iron. It was a perfect iron, but everyone didn't have one. In my husband's family they had a gas washer.

For a long time, we had gas stoves, and some people had oil stoves. Oil stoves get nice and hot.

The next thing we had was an Aladdin lamp with kerosene oil. You would light the mantle, and it gave a white light, much better for studying. We had one at the kitchen table where we did our homework. Our eyes adjusted to that kind of light. No one knew that electricity would make such a difference.

When I was a little girl I didn't think about it. What you don't have, you don't know. Before we had electricity, I used six dry cell batteries that I had to connect myself at the telegraph office.

We didn't have electric lights in Gabarus until February 9, 1947 when I was twenty-seven years old, married and a parent. Unbelievable how we lived before we got electricity. So many things changed overnight. Electricity was a marvel. Everyone had electricity at the same time. It changed our whole world. We could tear down the outdoor toilets. We all got indoor bathrooms, now that we had electricity to run the water pumps. Hot and cold water, washing machines, lights, radios that used to run on batteries. In the early days of the Telegraph Office in Gabarus, the woman operator had to make her own batteries out of mercury and lime. That was dangerous and difficult. With electricity, everything was so much easier. It made a huge difference. When we got lights everyone got a radio, and we knew what was going on in the outside world.

Seven Stores in Gabarus

When I was growing up in the 1920s and 30s there were seven stores in Gabarus, and they all made a living. We ate out of the store, and those store owners probably did too.

There wasn't really competition, since each store sold slightly different goods. Bill MacDonald had a store next to ours that sold fresh meat that he would get in Sydney. In my time, they took a horse and wagon to get supplies and later we used cars. The MacDonalds' little store was in front of their main house. That store from the MacDonalds' property is the small house next to the firehall now. The MacDonald's main house was originally on the beach, and it was moved to where it is now probably around late 1800s.

Among the seven stores in Gabarus, we had everything they had in Sydney. Grant Store was a general store. Another store specialized in selling gas. Another store sold souvenirs. There were another two or three general stores. What Grandpa didn't have the other store would. One of the last stores was up the road near the old Hill School.

Albert Bagnell, a captain of vessels, also had a store. He had different things than others. I think you had to ask for some things that were behind the counter. He also sold souvenirs. That store was on the property where Bruce Hardy lives now.

GRANT STORE WITH
UNCLE JIM REID CA. 1941.
MILDRED GRAY FAMILY
PHOTOGRAPH.
USED WITH PERMISSION.

Grant Store

The Grant Store was in the family 100 years. First, my great-grandfather William had the store, and then my grandfather, Captain John Grant, my father's father, took it over. My great-grandfather had another son, Abraham, who took over the store right down the street.

Originally, William Grant, my great-grandfather, had the store across from where the post office is now. After my grandfather Captain John Grant retired from being a sea captain in 1902 at the age of fifty-nine, he went into business with his father. He still caught fish and cured them himself, but mostly he worked at the store.

The building faced Memory Lane, just a few houses up from the beach and across the street from where we lived. The store was a two story building. Upstairs we had an ice cream parlor and a room to store caskets for my father and uncle's undertaking business. There was a barber shop down below and another shed with the puncheon of molasses.

Grant Store was a general store. We sold everything. The store was almost always open, except on Sundays. We would open at 8 and close at 9, but would often open up again if people needed something. This happened lots of times. One woman would always come when no one was there, around 10 p.m. My father would get what people needed, whenever they needed it.

In the store, a lot was on barter. It was the honor system. Lots of families were supported all winter by my grandfather, and sometimes they would pay with fish in the spring and summer or with money from selling their fish. Some couldn't pay, and some never paid. We priced things at 15% over the actual cost.

The store was a kind of community center too. Around 1902 the telegraph office was in the store. During World War I there was a Red Cross Club, a ladies' club that met in one of the rooms in the store where women would knit caps and mittens for the soldiers in the war.

You could buy anything at the store: hardware, fishing equipment…all household articles. In my day, they had cough syrup, shoes, kerosene oil, molasses, cheese, Vicks, soap, Rinso, Palmolive, Lifebuoy and cakes of soap for your face, window glass, yard goods, cotton by the yard, rubber boots, caskets, and at Christmas we had toys…and half wouldn't work because we had tried them out! Grandpa Grant would play with them too. Grandpa Captain Grant would always decorate the store for Christmas.

At that time, we got many goods from Halifax. My grandfather went in his own boat to get supplies in Halifax, and people would also pay him to take them to Halifax. Later, I remember a supply ship called the Halsyd coming into Gabarus from Halifax. It was named for Halifax-Sydney I think, "Hal" and "Syd." The supply boat would sound a horn when it went across the harbour. The boat was engine powered, and it used to come into Gabarus with supplies every three to four weeks until well into the 1960s. In the early days, my Grandpa Captain Grant was the agent for the boat. At that time, they would come into the breakwater, Government Wharf, over by the lighthouse, and they would transport the supplies to the seven stores in the village, usually with a horse and wagon until the 1930s when they started to use trucks more.

The kids would wait for the ship and go with someone on a wagon to pick up supplies at the wharf. It was a big outing, sitting on top of a box. Later, Grandpa Captain Grant used to hire Hal Crawley and his Ford car to meet the boat and bring the supplies back to the store. Part of the car was cut off, so it was more like an open bed truck.

We had fresh fruit in the store, bananas, apples and oranges. We bought bananas on stalks that came in a box. Daddy tied a string around the stalk and hung it up by the window. People liked bananas. One day Daddy caught a big spider on the bananas. We sent it somewhere to identify it. It was a tarantula.

We had Florida oranges, and apples came in barrels. On the top were big Gravenstein apples from the Annapolis Valley. They were packed in blue tissue paper. You could smell the apples through the paper! At that time most of the apples were big. They weren't graded at that time. No one has apples like that now. And they only cost 2 cents a pound. We also had berries in season. We never sold baked goods, since people made their own homemade bread and fruit pies and biscuits.

We always had lot of candy for sale in a showcase, like "Honeymoons" and "Old Fashioned Chocolates." We also sold "Garden Fruit Suckers", but chocolate was my favorite.

Grant Store was also a place for men's entertainment. Men sat around in the winter telling each other stories. They would talk about daily happenings, the news, and also about things that happened in the past. Many of the men would sit and whittle a stick with their knife. They weren't making it into a shape. They would just whittle down to nothing.

Every evening men would play checkers. Some wouldn't talk much, and some would talk a lot. They were all friends, mostly all fishermen. They were mostly older, but they were all ages too. That was their social life. Women would be home, taking care of the children or doing handiwork. For women, there was preserving to be done for the winter. And during the winter women hooked mats and knitted mittens, sweaters and hats for men to go fishing. One woman knitted underwear for her husband!

Men would sit around on the nail barrels until about 8 p.m. and talk, visit and play cards. There was a long church pew in the store. That was what they did, talk and play cards and checkers. People were happy.

The store was a place where the young people hung out too. You would buy a candy and communicate with everyone who was there. One day, a nine-year old boy from Grand Mira named Martin was at the store when the older boys and his friends were there too. Martin had brought out potatoes in a jute bag, and the boys were leaning up against the counter and the big boy pushed me to kiss Martin. They said "Let's make Mildred kiss Martin!" I was nine years old too. I was so embarrassed!

Everyone didn't have everything, but there was no business competition. If you couldn't find it at our store, you could buy something at another store. Each store had their own specialty, sold different things; Bill MacDonald next door to us sold fresh meat. In our store we sold only cured meats like bologna, sausage, and bacon, and we sold cheese--big wheels of cheese.

We used to sell gas from 45-gallon drums down at the beach. There was also a gas station at the end of the road where they pumped gas. After 1920, Grandpa Captain Grant sold gas for cars where the post office is right now. When people would come and get gas Grandpa would ask them to "take my little yellow-haired girl to the graveyard for a drive." It was a treat to go for a ride in a car. I was 4 or 5 years old. Gas was cheap in those days, less than 25 cents a gallon.

The road didn't end where it ends now. The road went to Gull Cove across the beach. In those days, most people were walking, not driving. Then they built the other road to the [Lakeview] cemetery, and people could go in cars. That was around the late 20s and early 1930s. I only heard of one car driving to Gull Cove on what we called the "grassy road" along the beach and the coast, probably in 1929. Horses and walking was the main thing.

When I was born we had someone hired to drive to Sydney to buy a whole lot of things for the store. We always had sausages that people really liked. They were 25 cents a pound. But generally we didn't sell meat. We always had fresh vegetables like cabbage, potatoes, turnips, carrots, but I never saw tomatoes until grade 11 when I went to Sydney to take my exams. I really liked tomatoes. Grandpa got them in the store, but not until around 1937. We didn't have broccoli or cauliflower and probably wouldn't know how to cook them. We had the basic foods and lots of them. All through my life we had a store. We always had food.

My niece Lillian Harriss reminded me that starting in 1936 we had a weather bulletin put on a post by Grant Store, and there was also one on the post at the Methodist Church crossroads in a homemade wood frame with a glass front. It was posted around 7 a.m. and 1 p.m. everyday. The weather reports came in by radio at 1 a.m. and 1 p.m. and then were posted by Dan Stewart's wife Myrtle on the bulletin boards.

Dan Stewart's radio was brought out to him by a small 2-seater airplane owned by his friend Reg Roger. This was a wonderful convenience for the people of the village as radios were few here. John Gray, Duncan's father, had the first radio in Gabarus.

People got most of their information about the outside world in the daily newspaper. People were well informed. Also, everybody got the Family Herald. It was a western magazine, very informative. You would find out how people were living in the west. It was Canada's farm magazine. There was one page in that publication called the "Maple Leaf Page" for children looking for pen pals. My pen pal and I corresponded from the time we were 12. She lived in Kings County, Nova Scotia, Pleasant River. We never met, but we wrote back and forth for years.

Puncheon of Molasses

One of the most vivid recollections of my childhood was of the puncheon of molasses that we always had at the store. The Gabarus sea captains who traveled to Barbados with fish would bring back a puncheon of molasses. A puncheon was a large wooden barrel made in the West Indies that held more than 90 gallons of molasses. It was as big as more than two barrels which hold 45 gallons each. It was very very heavy, around 1170 pounds with molasses weighing 13 pounds a gallon.

When the vessel came in from Barbados with the puncheon of molasses at the Government Wharf in Gabarus it must have been hard to get it off the ship. It was so heavy. My grandfather Grant would carry it on a horse and wagon to get it to the store. Then they would roll it in on boards. There was a double door going into the back shed. It took three or four men to do it.

When it arrived the puncheon was airtight. My grandfather made a hole to put the pump in with a brace and bit and cut it out with his knife. Sometimes there would be wood chips in the molasses. There was a corking type filler between the stays of the barrel. My Grandpa Grant also sold cork in the store. It came from Portugal to Halifax. You may know that cork is from the bark of a tree that grows in Portugal and Spain, not the first bark, the second bark.

There was a pump in the barrel from which we could pump and sell the molasses by the pint or quart. I think it was 25 cents a quart. We were on imperial then. One puncheon in our store would last at least a year. In those days everyone bought molasses and used it for cooking. I don't think molasses freezes. When the puncheon was empty there would be at least three inches of the brown sugar at the bottom. It was so delicious. We had that at the house, and we used to put it on ice cream, or snow, depending on the season.

When it was empty we would sell the puncheon to a fisherman to cure his mackerel and codfish with salt before he would dry them on flakes outdoors. At that time the women would spread the salted fish out to dry. It was one of the jobs the women did.

Later, the supply ship Halsyd would bring in the puncheon of molasses.

Coal and Kerosene

In our store, the coal was next to the puncheon. The coal was only for the pot-bellied stove to heat the store. The coal would come from Glace Bay on a truck. I recall that they sold it by the ton. When the truck arrived, they would shovel it off the truck into the corner of the store. There was a puncheon of molasses next to it and kerosene in another corner. We sold kerosene oil that people used for their lamps. People would buy it by the gallon or half gallon. A gallon would last, depending on how much they used, and how many lamps they had, perhaps a week. It cost 25 cents a gallon as I recall. It was not very sanitary. There was a pump on the can. Luckily no one got poisoned or burned.

Dan and Myrtle Stewart

GRAY FAMILY WITH ICE BOAT
LEFT TO RIGHT
DUNCAN, RALPH, MYRTLE, EDITH, KENNETH, AND JOE. CA. 1940 FROM THE COLLECTION OF LILLIAN AND KATHY HARRISS.
USED WITH PERMISSION.

Lillian Harriss' father, Dan Stewart, was the barber at the Grant Store. He was a very very nice man. He worked as a glazier for the government at Point Edward naval base, but worked as a barber on the side. Dan was a veteran of World War I. He was at the battle of Passchendaele on the Western Front during the war. Trench warfare is grueling, so he must have experienced some really difficult times, but he never talked about it. Lillian's brother Emerson has been my brother Ken's best friend from childhood.

Lillian's mother Myrtle was [my husband] Duncan's sister. Myrtle took her nurse training at the Halifax hospital, and when she came back to Gabarus, she helped a lot of people who were ill. She gave needles [shots] and helped deliver many babies. She helped anyone who was sick, and she did it all for free. Myrtle worked closely with the doctor, different doctors who had patients here. They could depend on her to tell them what was going on and to give pain medications. She helped so many people. She was ninety-three when she died. Myrtle lived a couple of houses away from us.

LEFT TO RIGHT
EMERSON STEWART AND KENNETH GRANT. CA. 1940. MILDRED GRAY FAMILY PHOTOGRAPH.
USED WITH PERMISSION.

Lillian's brother Emerson and sisters Shirley and Gwen lived in Gabarus most of their childhood. They went different places to work and live, and Lillian worked in Sydney before she married Albert Harriss and moved back to Gabarus. Shirley and Gwen were both nurses, and Emerson was an administrator in the hospital in New Glasgow.

74   Bringing Out the Untold Life

MILDRED'S FATHER WILEY GRANT. CA. 1925. MILDRED GRAY FAMILY PHOTOGRAPH. USED WITH PERMISSION.

Grant and Reid Undertakers

Daddy was a Justice of the Peace. So was my Uncle John Reid, my mother's brother. Grant and Reid was also the name of their undertaking business. Daddy and Uncle John had no education in the undertaking business. In those days, the job of undertaker consisted mainly of making sure the funeral was organized and all the details were taken care of, filling out the paperwork for the authorities, "laying people out", dressing them and getting them ready for the casket. Every family has their own plot, and people always knew where they would be buried. Herman Bagnell had the authority to do the death certificate. He was also the secretary of the school. My father and my Uncle John would coordinate the funeral with the minister. The minister was usually with the person when they died.

Daddy sold caskets until 1954 when he sold the store and the business. The caskets were kept on the second floor of the store and brought down after they were purchased and taken to the home of the person who died. They sold them for the whole area. The caskets were in wooden boxes, piled one on top of the other. We used to play around them when we were kids. It was a good place to play hide and seek.

As the undertaker my father would carve the person's name, date of birth and date of death on a lead breastplate of about 3 x 6 inches that was attached to the top of the caskets. My father's writing was so beautiful. He wrote with an English script. Daddy would use a three-sided file, a special carpenter's file with a point on it, that he used to carve the names in the soft lead of the breastplate. Sometimes, people would use them as souvenirs.

They used to buy caskets from Montague in Prince Edward Island. That company is still in business. At the time, the caskets sold for $85 for the nicest ones with brocade covering. The plain ones were $65. He also sold fittings (handles, hinges, breastplates) for people who wanted to make their own caskets. Daddy also had excelsior for the bedding pad. Often he would sew the covering himself.

Daddy never built the adult caskets, only the baby ones that he could make out of an old box that he covered with fabric. We felt so bad when a baby died. Daddy filled the satin liner with excelsior, like dry straw, and then used thumbtacks that looked like stars to secure it. Now most people die in the hospital or hospice, but in those days a lot of people died at home, and they wanted to die here. Everyone did pretty much the same things after a family member died, regardless of their religion. Close friends and family would come together to grieve and talk about the life of the person who died.

When anyone died, daddy had an artificial "spray" that would be attached to the door of the home where the person died. It was two palm leaves together and artificial flowers in the middle. If anyone saw that, they knew that someone in that home had died. It would be on the house for three days until after the funeral.

In those days, when people died, the family would keep the body at home until the services and the burial. There was an open casket at the service. Close relatives would stay up all night while the body was in the house, so that the dead person wouldn't be alone. I don't think they had prayers in the night unless individual family members wanted to, although the minister would come. After two to three days the body would be taken to the church for the service. My family was Methodist, but there were other denominations in Gabarus: Catholic, Baptist, Presbyterian, and they all had similar death rituals. Most of the Catholics would be buried in Grand Mira. There were not that many Catholics in Gabarus. After the funeral, there would be a tea lunch at the church which was kind of a social event, a bit like it is now.

The common causes of death were TB and cancer of different kinds. There was no treatment for cancer then, none at all. A lot of my relatives in the earlier years died from TB, and children would sometimes die of childhood diseases or TB. TB would run through families.

The local people would go and dig the grave by hand. Since there was no embalming then, people had to be buried within two or three days. In the winter graves were still dug by hand using a pick and shovel. Everyone would be helping, and it was hard. People would say: "We have some hard digging today!" Winter or summer, they had to dig the hole 6 feet deep.

Orange Lodge

The natives of Gabarus were mostly Methodists. In Grand Mira, it was mostly Catholic. They would come to the store, and Grammy Grant would have them to tea. We never had any discrimination, but some people had.

The Orange Lodge was all Protestant, and the Knights of Columbus all Catholics. Grandpa Captain Grant also belonged to the Masons. That was just for men. They had a picture of the crest of the three chains. In Framboise there is still a Masons' organization.

The Orange Lodge was only men, only Protestant. They had to pay dues. They did a lot of work including maintaining the [community] hall. This was before my time.

Sir Charles Tupper must have been a member of the Orange Lodge. He was out speaking in different communities looking for votes. Through Grandpa Grant, Charles Tupper gave seventy-five chairs to the Orange Lodge. It was a big thing at the time. When they dissolved I bought one for $5, a small kitchen chair.

The Orange Lodge was against other religions, an organization against Catholics. They may still have it in Newfoundland. There was another organization called the True Blues for men and women. They helped people who needed help.

At that time, everyone in Gabarus belonged to the Orange Lodge, people from adjoining villages too, especially Fourchu. The Orange Lodge dissolved when the [second world] war was on, and young people were away. People were more enlightened, not so exclusive.

There was once an ornate organ in the hall. The Orange Lodge gave the building to the church, [Gabarus United], and then the church gave it to the village.

Mid-Winter Orange Drive

In the middle of winter, a big thing in the village would be an "Orange Drive." It was a parade of decorated horse-drawn sleighs. I remember so well Daddy making the decorations. The event was on February 12 unless it was storming. Then they might change the date. I was too young when this was going on in the 1920s. Everyone gathered at the hall, and then went for a drive to Gabarus Lake and then Fourchu. There were about ten horses and sleighs. And people in those villages came to Gabarus for the Drive. It was all over by the time I was old enough to go.

We had a lot more snow then. Anyone with a girlfriend would take them in a sleigh that would be decorated with streamers, big ribbons of orange and white. The blowing of the streamers scared some of the horses, and they would run ahead of the others.

In the evening, there was a supper, pie social, and square dance. Waltzing was the in thing then. There was live music with local musicians performing, mostly fast tunes on the piano, but some played the guitar or violin. In those days, a lot of people played the piano. Someone from Gabarus Lake may have played the fiddle. At the time, we all called it a violin. As far as I know a fiddle and a violin are the same instrument. The difference is the type of music played on it. They played fast highland tunes.

Girls made pies without their names. The pies were all decorated with paper roses. There was a competition to bid on their pies, and the man who bought the pie would get to eat the pie with the person who made it. It was a very competitive, an old-fashioned way of courting, and it made money for the Orange Lodge. Fellows and their girlfriends and married people went too. My aunts and their boyfriends would go. My mother and father went on it. Anyone could go, but it was usually young couples who did square dancing after the pie social. They rode in a fancy sleigh, not the kind for bringing wood home.

Doctor in the Village

For most of the years of my childhood, we had a doctor in the village. Dr. George Hutchinson came here, and when he became a widower, he married a lady from here. He was here when Duncan was 15, and he operated on Duncan's appendix. Dr. Hutchinson was my father's generation, probably born around 1885. Not sure when he came, but in time to deliver me at home in 1920. That I know.

Dr. Hutchinson's wife had one child and then died in childbirth with the second. Shortly after her death, he delivered a baby girl. During the birth, the mother of that baby said "Be very careful of the baby, because she may be your wife one day!" Sure enough, he married this woman, and they had five more children. Dr. Hutchinson's one child from his first wife was a friend of the girl he married. They got along really well.

Dr. Hutchinson was here a long time. He built his own house and practiced in Gabarus for at least 30 years. He lived in the big house across from the community hall. He left here years later when he went to serve as a doctor on ships. I think he died on a ship. Their youngest son visited last year. He is 75 now.

There was another doctor, Dr. Alexander, a black man. He was before Dr. Hutchinson. He was a GP I think. He was a traveling doctor. He would be here for a while before the 1920s. Dr. Alexander performed surgery on my great uncle on the kitchen table. He had appendicitis which was a real threat then. They used chloroform as an anesthetic. It probably wasn't that uncommon. He is the only one I can think of. Dr. Alexander's wife is buried in the Lakeview Cemetery.

Duncan's sister Myrtle who was the mother of Lillian Harriss, Emerson Stewart, Shirley Horne and Gwen Teal, also helped deliver babies. Myrtle had trained as a nurse in Halifax. Myrtle helped a lot of people. She would call the doctor to get instructions. If anyone was sick, they would send for her to come.

There was also a traveling dentist who would come so many times a year. The dentist would stay at least a week. There was not a lot of filling teeth, mostly extractions. I have some teeth filled from that dentist, fillings that lasted my whole life. I had two fillings replaced just this year. The old fillings had been put in more than seventy years ago!

In 1918, shortly before I was born, there was a flu epidemic in the area, and a lot of people died, especially people who were having babies. Before we had a doctor, childbirth was usually helped by a midwife. There were not a lot of deaths in childbirth, maybe one or two. In those days (1920s), TB or pneumonia was the main cause of children dying young. I remember two or three babies dying over a 5 year period when I was a little girl. It was not common.

In the winter of 1936 I needed a doctor myself. Dr. Hutchinson said I had appendicitis, and I had to have surgery. I was sixteen years old. It was a long journey to Sydney. We left Gabarus at 8 a.m. in a horse-drawn sleigh, just me and my mother and the driver. The sleigh was like a box. Elsie was sitting up, and I was lying down. I was covered in hot water bottles and blankets. The snow was very deep, and the horse had to go up off the road. We arrived at the hospital in Sydney at 8 p.m. I had my appendix out that night. Now that journey takes about 35 minutes in a car.

In the winter of February 1938, when my sister Freda was in nurse's training, she had the measles and had to get to the hospital, but again the road was blocked with snow. Fortunately, a man who had an airplane was bringing a radio to the Grays, and Freda was able to go to the hospital with him. So he was there when needed.

Since the plane was only a two-seater, another girl, Sadie MacDonald, "Mac", who was also a nurse at the hospital, had to wait for the plane to come back for her. The airplane landed on "The Level" (near where the Methodist Church used to be on the Upper Barrachois). He charged $20 for the trip. When the weather was nice, sometimes he would take people up in the plane over the village for $5, but the first time I was on an airplane was in 1947 when I was called home from Boston because my Uncle Herb died.

Grant Property - Waiting for Mailman. 1944. Photographer Unknown. Item Number 89-1216-19407. Beaton Institute, Cape Breton University.

Mail Delivery and Early Automobiles in Gabarus

We never had a car when I was growing up. Most of the time we didn't need one. We used a horse and covered carriage or wagon. When I was little a lot of the supplies came in by boat. If we needed a car, my father used to hire a car to get groceries for the store. When we were married in 1941 Duncan and I couldn't afford a car. I didn't drive myself until much later.

One man in the village named Dan MacLeod had a car. He was the person my mother and Aunt Jemima hired to take us to Sydney each summer. He hired his car to other people too. People in the village would also take others in or out of town. We had a bus that went to Sydney in the morning and returned in the evening for 10 years starting in 1939.

The road was not paved until 1955. Duncan MacDougall delivered the mail to Gabarus every day except Sunday in a horse and wagon. Then he had a 1942 Ford panel truck. In those days he would give rides (like a bus) and delivered groceries too. He charged a little. If the road was blocked or if the pothole was too big, Duncan would stop, cut down a tree to fill the hole, and drive on.

Outings to Sydney and Vidol Hotel

When I was growing up, we went to Sydney once a year. It was like someone telling me today to go to France. Now folks go three times a day and think don't think anything of it. Those 36 kilometers might as well have been thousands.

In the summer, my mother Elsie and my Aunt Jemima would hire a car to take us to town for the day. It was a day to remember and plan and think about. A lot of kids didn't get to go to Sydney.

We got a hotel room at the Vidol Hotel at the corner of Dorchester and Charlotte for the day for $1. We would stay at the hotel until 4 p.m. The hotel had bathrooms. It was a novelty to us, since at the time we didn't have toilets in Gabarus. It was fun to flush the toilet. We went to Woolworth's 5 and 10 to buy all kinds of stuff. I was given 25 cents from my Grammy Reid, 15 cents from my Grandpa Reid, and a dollar from my Grant grandparents. Freda would get $1 more. I could have up to $3 if I saved a bit. In those days $3 bought a lot. I remember buying a cash box with a tray. We'd come home with our little gifts we bought. We used to make this trip once over each summer. We went to a restaurant for dinner. It was a wonderful thing to go to a restaurant. They had great hot dog rolls. They were so good we brought some home. The Vidol Hotel has been torn down.

GABARUS PRIMARY WITH TEACHER MARJORIE MACGILLIVARY IN BLACK CLOCHE HAT IN 1930 AND MILDRED GRANT IN LEFT CORNER THIRD FROM THE LEFT. MILDRED GRAY FAMILY PHOTOGRAPH.
USED WITH PERMISSION.

School Days

In those days teachers had great authority. They were not friendly or familiar. They were a niche above. You would never call a teacher by their first name, even if she lived in your home. You would never dare chew gum in school. You always had to call them miss this and miss that and mister this and mister that.

Most of our teachers were "from away." They would board at people's houses. In Gabarus, there were two men teachers, one from North Sydney, and one from the Annapolis Valley. Mabel Lees boarded at our home and was my teacher in second grade. She was a young girl, about 19 or 20.

My favorite teacher was Marjorie MacGillivary Reid. She was my teacher in grade four. She grew up on Rouse Island and married young, 20 or 21, I think. Marjorie married a fisherman. They were very much in love. I remember her being an excellent teacher. Her whole life she had the same hairstyle she had when she was my teacher. In those days, teachers were demanding. Marjorie died this year just after her 101st birthday. Marjorie was a very fine person. I talked with her on the phone every day. She was still interested in everything. She was bright and engaged.

Our neighbors Vivian and Eunice both taught school too. School was serious business, not a lot of fun or fooling around. The teachers gave the lessons and did the discipline. We had to be respectful to the teachers, since they were just like ministers and elders.

I hated school. I liked the teachers, but they had a strap, and they could discipline kids. Their job was to teach children etiquette and respect. We were all frightened of the teacher. The teachers could strap the students if they were bad. They would whack your hand. They had a pointer, and they could hit you with that. This happened every day. Especially the boys would get in trouble.

We went to school in all kinds of weather, and the teacher was always there. We had school no matter the weather, or we had to go on Saturday to make up for it. Most of us walked. We would go to school through the fields. Teachers could walk to school too. I can't remember school being cancelled because of the weather like it is now.

I had a kidney condition when I was little, so I started school a year late. I was six when I started school about halfway through the year, and Daddy took me on his back during a snow storm. At the school, there was a coal-burning stove in the middle of the floor. The boys would look after it. It burned with a good flame, and it burned pretty clean. There was a stove in each of the two rooms. The boys would stir the coal with a broom handle and then run around and chase the girls with it.

My first school was only a few doors away from where I live now. I started there. In 1936 the new school was built, so I went there in grade 10 and 11. That is a house now, but that was a school until 10 years or so ago. It was a two-room school house. One room was for grades 1-6, with grades 7-11 in the other. When I was young, we had double desks with two children sitting together. At the new school that was built in 1936 we had single desks.

There were about sixty students in the whole school, all ages to 11th grade. A lot of professionals came out of our little school like ministers and doctors. Four of us started school together Everett Bagnell, Albert MacDonald, Edna MacGillivary and me. When Albert came back from the war, he took a degree in business administration. Edna got married when the war was on, Everett was in the war too, in the Canadian Navy, and he landed at Normandy. When he came back he worked at the Steel Plant in Sydney. They have all passed away now, but we were the best of friends.

There was one short recess at 10:15, and if it wasn't raining or snowing we went out to play. There were no electric lights at the school then. We had to get out of school by 3 p.m. to get home by dark. I went to grade 1-11 in two different rooms.

There were dahlias and gladiolas at the school that the children planted. Now there are also peonies and narcissus growing wild in places where they were once cultivated by the students. Once a year on Arbor Day in May we had to clean the school thoroughly, the desks, blackboard. It was a lot of fun too. We chased each other around with blackboard brushes full of chalk.

When I was a child in school I always thought that others were smarter than I. I had a kind of an inferiority complex. But no one ever said "You are a girl. You are not smart." If I wanted to become a doctor, that would have been fine. People would be glad you had the intellect or the money to become a doctor or a professional. My family always tried to put me up, but I wasn't as smart as my sister Freda. She was a great student. She won prizes. I never won a prize in my life.

Childhood Games

When we were children, we made our own entertainment. You had to make your own natural type of entertainment. That is a good way. You become a more resourceful person, especially good for children. In a place like Gabarus, there is more variety of natural entertainment.

In the winter there was lots of sledding on hills during the day. There were not many trees then. We would coast down and walk back. In those days we had a lot of snow, and we made snow houses, and had hockey games. That was before the war.

During the summer we were at the beach all the time, swimming, jumping off the wharf and playing on the beach. Sometimes we went out with Daddy when he went out fishing.

We played a lot of games, many of our own creation. In school, we used to play games on the porch like "Pussy in the Corner." I am not sure if it was one we made up or a general game. We would run from one corner to the other, and the person in the center would try to take our place. They would take the hand of the person in the opposite corner. Odd man out went into the center. Outside we played hide and seek, and tag. We played a lot of tag, especially around the school.

We played ball, and jack knives was popular. We played this at school. The boys mostly had knives, but girls would borrow them. You needed a pocket knife to play and also a board or a wood plank. The schoolhouse steps worked well. The knife was unfolded halfway, and we would flip the knife to see which way it would land. We dropped it on the board rather than throwing it. Flat was so many points. The game was very popular with boys, but a lot of us girls played it too, and we didn't get in trouble for playing it. We knelt down. It was not like throwing a knife or anything. Boys were better at it than most of the girls, but my friend Margaret was very good at it. Only two could play at a time. We also played "king" on good days. In that game, there were four or five children on each side, and the object was to take another's place.

At home, we played games too, mostly card games and board games like Old Maid, Parcheesi, Chinese Checkers and regular checkers. Birthday parties were always special, and we played lots of games like Pin the Tail on the Donkey and Red Rover. We always had cake with candles and little goodies, and we played games. I remember my 10th birthday. There were ten people. We had cookies, candy, and lime juice.

When my children were little in the evenings we played games too. We didn't play cards, since Duncan's mother thought cards were the Devil's work. Cards were not allowed in her home. We played Chutes and Ladders, Chinese Checkers, and we played Monopoly a lot.

In our small community we used to share traditional holidays. In my day, Christmas was more sacred, and there were a lot of shared experiences like caroling. I believe that traditional things make you feel better about yourself and your role in the community.

When I was growing up we had a lot of fun with storytelling. My father would make up stories when I was little. We had two cats, Kip, a Tom cat, and Bubbles, a she cat. Daddy used to make up stories about Kip and Bubbles having a big party, inviting all their cat friends and getting into the molasses puncheon at the store. If my father was lying down, my cousin Jean and I used to put doll clothes on my father's feet. He would pretend the dolls on his feet were going to a dance. It was natural imaginative fun. Daddy would sometimes make fudge and play with us.

Now children don't have natural play. All they know is TV and video games. They won't have anything to reminisce about. When they look back on their life, what will they remember?

Earthquake of 1929

When I was nine years old, on November 14, 1929, there was an earthquake and tidal wave in Gabarus. Now they would call it a tsunami. When it happened late in the afternoon, I was coming up to the house from feeding the pig at the barn which was a couple of doors away from my house. People were outside. The earthquake lasted five minutes with two tremors, and then we thought it was over. But the tidal wave hit after dark at 8 p.m. At that time we had no street lights. The wave destroyed a lot of fishing equipment on the beach, also fish houses, and it really changed the shape of the land. Before the earthquake there was no eel grass growing in the barachois; now it is growing in abundance. There was a lot of flooding. The water went up to the first few houses off the beach. You had to row a boat to those homes. It changed the whole area at the beach, and a lot of fishing moved. It made the barachois much smaller.

LEFT TO RIGHT
WILEY GRANT, MILTON SUTHERLAND, ELIAS SHERWOOD, DAN STEWART. CA. 1954. MILDRED GRAY FAMILY PHOTOGRAPH.
USED WITH PERMISSION.

Cutting the Ice

In our family, we always had ice, and lime juice was the drink back when we were young. We bought it by the bottle and mixed it with water: a tablespoon of lime juice, sugar, water and ice. There were no additives. It was a great summer drink.

Ice came from the ice saved from the winter. In the winter, in the month of March, Daddy would cut ice out of the little pond on Gull Cove Road. Now I would not eat ice from that lake. It might be as clean, but it would be saltier.

Men used to work with him that day. There were three besides Daddy: Townsend, Sherwood, and the other man who ran the horse. One man would have a horse, and two were cutters. They used an ice saw to cut it in 18 inch cubes that they would take to our ice house.

It took two days to cut it and one day to haul it to the ice house. It was a good day's work. The men all lived in the village near us. They lived behind us and across the road, and they had the ice saw.

It was dangerous work. They had to stand on the ice and carve the ice around their feet. Once they got a few pieces cut they had to pull it onto the ice. The men helped put it on the sleigh, and they used ice hooks to move it into the ice house. In the ice house, the ice was packed in sawdust that came in bags from one of the nearby sawmills. We would put down a layer of ice, then sawdust. It would stick together. Packed in sawdust, that ice would last all summer.

In those days, we cut it on the ocean side. It was pure; no one got sick from it. At the end of the big day of work cutting the ice, Elsie would have a pot of corned pork and all kinds of vegetables and apple pie for dessert. This was a wonderful day, and all the men came for dinner.

It was a big job, but it was so nice to have ice in the summer. When we put the ice in our drinks, sometimes a little sawdust would come to the surface, but we didn't care.

Prohibition Adventures

In Gabarus, we had a prevention officer who was looking out for rum runners coming into the harbour. This was in the 1930s when there were a lot of "rum runners" during prohibition coming in to sell liquor, in kegs, by boat.

The officer was boarding at a home in Gabarus. Anyone he would catch would get in trouble. Over on the north shore of Gabarus Bay some people got caught and another in Framboise and along the coast. It was a violent business, very secretive, hush hush. It was dangerous to mention anyone in connection with rum running. Everyone minded their own business.

On the North Shore, an Italian was caught taking liquor off a boat. He swam under the boat when the prevention officers showed up. The man swam to Harbour Rock, but they caught him later.

Music and Community Life

We had a piano, and my mother Elsie played. She had taken lessons and also taught herself. In those days, more people had organs than pianos. Once there was a minister here, Rev. Hobbs, and his wife was a trained singer. She trained a lot of people. When the war was on, after church, people would come down to our home and listen to Gabriel Heatter on the radio. He had a service later than ours, a sermon and choir too. The program was from Buffalo, New York, which was the end of the world as far as I was concerned.

People would listen and enjoy the music. Elsie couldn't sing, and she was shy about playing our piano when more skilled accompanists were around. Our church had a lovely choir of about eight or ten people. They were all very good singers. A couple of ladies would play the piano at church and later at our house for the sing-songs. We sang hymns. One of my favorite hymns is Softly and Tenderly, Jesus is Calling. In the Garden is what Elsie wanted sung at her funeral, but the singer didn't get here to sing it.

Between Sunday School, church services and the sing-songs over my whole lifetime, I know the words to almost every hymn in the hymn book. I also know the tune of almost every hymn. My most favorite hymn is Abide with Me, a prayer for God to remain present throughout life, through trials and tragedy, and through death: *Abide with me; ... Lord, with me abide. When other helpers fail and comforts flee ... I need thy presence every passing hour...Through cloud and sunshine, Lord, abide with me. I fear no foe, with thee at hand to bless; ills have no weight, and tears not bitterness. ... in life, in death, O Lord, abide with me.*

In later years, when we were teenagers, the boys from Fourchu and Belfry used to come to church to see the girls down here. There wasn't much to do on Sundays, not at all. But you could walk to the boardwalk just to be together with other young people.

In those days, around the mid-1930s, there was really no such thing as a "boyfriend." One time when I came home from a walk; a boy had his arm around me. My mother was on the veranda with a friend in a hammock, and she said "Is that you Middie? It's going on nine." Not much chance of her not knowing it was me! It was still light. He was not serious. I must have been 16. "Don't forget, you have to be home by 9!" My parents, all parents in those days, were very protective.

Now, there is no Sunday church school, and the minister has a different role. I think a little more respect for people in authority would help people today. I worry that there is too much violence on TV. Many children cannot separate fact from fantasy. Some of the kids don't know that what they see is just acting.

Dance on Crazy Horse Bridge

When we were teenagers we were not supposed to go very far from home. I was not allowed out after 8 p.m. at night. But one beautiful summer night a group of us young people were walking around, and we decided to have a dance. We walked up to Crazy Brook Bridge on the old road along the water which was right next to Slattery Lake, only about a half mile from the village but still off limits. It was a no-no to go that far from home. Charlie Shepherd from Fourchu played a mouth organ. He used to work in the lobster factory. The bridge was about 10 feet square, and at night it was totally deserted, a great place to dance. We used to waltz and fox trot to the music of the harmonica. There was a man who played the accordion. I don't think any of us got in any trouble.

Church Life in Gabarus

In the early 1800s the nearest church and clergyman was in Sydney, St. George's that was built in the late 1700s, so if you wanted to get married you had to travel on horseback or walk on a road that was mostly a path through the woods. My great-grandparents Mary and William Grant and my own parents had to make the trek. My great-grandparents William and Mary Grant walked all the way 26 miles [42 km]. My parents went in a horse-drawn sleigh.

In the 1800s there was a lot going on in the Methodist community. A man named William Charlton came to Cape Breton in the early 1800s. After he married a woman from Louisbourg, Ann Townsend, they settled in Gabarus. After a few years they moved to Boston, where they were both converted to Methodism under the preaching of a Methodist evangelist [Elijah Henning]. Charlton became a preacher, and they moved back to Gabarus. Charlton preached the gospel to the people in Gabarus until his death in 1838. He converted a lot of people. He was responsible for a lot of revival meetings. William Charlton changed people to Methodist. I think that Charlton may be buried in the old cemetery. I know that there was a plaque to him at the church.

I think that Rev. Howie was the first resident minister in the 1800s. The Methodist church construction was started in 1858 by people in the community, many of whom were shipbuilders. The bottom part was made of logs out of a ship. About forty years ago, they replaced the old windows; my niece Sandra bought one of the old ones, and she made a mirror out of the back and used the original frame. Beautiful.

The old-time minister was the nucleus of the community. The minister was a much honored person, central to the well-being of the community. Ministers were prominent people in those days. People would name their babies after the minister or want to. If the minister or priest was coming to your home it was a big deal. If the minister was coming you had to open up the parlor. The minister was the first person you called if you were sick or in trouble.

WESLEY UNITED CHURCH OF GABARUS CA. 1980. MILDRED GRAY FAMILY PHOTOGRAPH. USED WITH PERMISSION.

We had a lot of ministers from England. The minister when I was a child was Rev. Nightingale. I was christened by him. Minister Nightingale had a manse. It was just torn down a couple of years ago. There were several different ministers when I was growing up including Rev. MacKillop who married the telegraph operator Christina Grant.

Gabarus Lake was Presbyterian, and our church, Wesley United in Gabarus, was Methodist. In my day, all of the services were in English. A few ladies from Gabarus Lake spoke Gaelic but not in Gabarus or Fourchu.

In 1925, the United Church of Canada was founded when the three churches came together, Methodist, Presbyterian and Congregationalist. When it happened, I think the Methodist Church in Gabarus was still on its own, but about 15 years ago the church was closed, sold and moved from the spot where it had been. When the Protestant churches were joined together not everyone was for it. They still had the Methodist ideas. Many never really gave up their individual denomination. Even to this day.

In 1900 there were more than 1,000 people to support the churches which were the center of village life. In those days, all communities revolved around the Church. It was a disaster when the church closed.

When I was growing up the church was definitely the nucleus of the village. We had Sunday school and lots of activities at the church: Strawberry Festival, Easter Tea, Christmas Concert, and the Summer Picnic.

We went to church here in the morning, 10 am on Sunday prayer meeting if you were old enough. Teenagers were old enough. And there was prayer meeting on Wednesday night.

The whole Sunday was full of church activities:
Starting at 7 a.m. Have breakfast and get ready to go to church
10 a.m.   Bible study
11 a.m.   Church
Noon   Church out
           We took off our Sunday clothes and ate dinner
2:00 p.m. Dress up again, go to Sunday School
3:00 p.m. Home, Elsie started supper
7-8 p.m.   Back to church if you were old enough (little kids, under 6, stayed home)

We were never allowed to do anything else on Sunday, no swimming, skating, coasting, no playing games or cards. After 3 p.m. you could go pick flowers or you could go for a walk, but after supper there was more church, and then it was time to go to bed.

Through the church there was Ladies' Aid, and some of the upkeep was taken care of by the Ladies' Auxiliary. Ladies met once a week to make things to sell at the church to support the church programs. The children had groups too. We had a Mission Circle for our Methodist Church that helped maintain the church and for missionary work. I was involved with the Mission Circle for many years, all through my teens. I was president. We made clothes for babies and poor people in the area and collected used stamps, cards, sent money to foreign countries for missions and orphans in Africa during the civil war in Biafra. More recently, we were collecting eyeglasses for people who needed glasses. Eventually, Mission Circle dissolved since there were not enough members, especially after the church closed in 1997. It was a really nice group of women who worked together.

In summer there was always a big Sunday school picnic with children of all ages. We went down to Ram's Head beach on the grassy road on the way to Gull Cove and Second Lake Beach. That is where we had the picnic. We all walked there on the Gull Cove Road. We used to look forward to that all year.

Over thirty children and adults participated. There were games and prizes. Women would put a sheet down on the ground. Daddy made swings on the trees. We used to play tag, swing and get little prizes. We stopped doing it when I was about twelve years old.

When I was growing up almost everyone was Methodist and went to church. Besides our church, the churches that I knew about were the Methodist churches at Gull Cove, Irish Brook and Big Cape, after Gull Cove. Now only about a half dozen families from Gabarus go to the new combined church of Zion (Gabarus Lake) and Wesley (Gabarus) from here.

Over near the lighthouse there was a Catholic Church that was built around 1902. There is a funny story about the lobster broker, Mr. Slattery, who was a Catholic and my grandfather Captain Grant traveling to Halifax to buy bricks for the church. At that time there were quite a few Catholics. Around the first siege of Louisbourg the settlers were Catholic, and a lot of Catholics worked in the lobster factories. In my time, Catholics were moving away, and there weren't so many, especially when there was no industry, after the lobster factories closed at the Cape, Gull Cove, and in Gabarus. I do remember when I was little there was always a Catholic mass on Christmas Eve, and we used to take a friend whose mother was Catholic. The last church closed after I was grown up, after the war, I think around the 1960s. The Catholic Church was moved to Sydney and converted to a house.

There was also a Baptist Church towards the lighthouse on the left on the hill on the bank on the old road that ran along the ocean. That church was there until about the 1930s. It closed and then fell down.

Christmas Concert, Highlight of the Winter

The Christmas concerts of my childhood were even more wonderful without electric lights. We practiced by the light of the hanging kerosene lamps. It would have been hard to take pictures then, since it was so dark. The pictures of those days are in the mind's eye, in our memories which are vivid and abiding.

In the church, we would be at practice for a little while every day to go over our recitation. The church had a coal burning furnace and one register in the middle of the floor. It would usually be warm. We didn't mind the cold anyway. I just loved those Christmas concerts. In my day it really meant a lot. It was not commercialized. Not at all.

The Christmas concert was the highlight of the winter. It took place at the church and started at 7 p.m. a couple of days before Christmas. During the Christmas Concert, the church would be full of people, even up in the balcony. All the parents were there. There was a nativity scene in it and a guiding star. Mary Bagnell was the star. She carried a wand with a star. For the occasion, all the girls had new dresses and the boys had new suits. All the children made recitations, and everyone was so proud of their children. Each year, one child did a monologue. I was too shy to do that. Some girls would sing Away in a Manger.

The center of the scene was the drill. It was the highlight of the event. For the drills ten children would form a star and other pairings. All the girls wore a white crepe paper dress with a sash of green or red. In the Eastern Star drill, there was a pole wand covered with aluminum foil with a star at the top. All the children carried stars on a wand covered with aluminum foil. My Grandpa Grant used to get tea in big cube boxes, about 1.5 foot cubes. There was aluminum foil on top of the tea boxes, and he would save it for the Christmas concert. It was used to make the stars and to cover the handle of the pole for the Eastern Star. With the kerosene lamps shining on the stars and tinsel it was beautiful. At the end of the concert, the head girl sang Star of the East.

They would have a Christmas tree that my father would have already decorated. Since there were no electric lights, he would make garlands out of different colors of tissue paper that he would cut into pieces about 4 inches x 1 inch and then use mucilage to glue the two ends together to make a chain garland.

Santa Claus would come to the Christmas Concert. My father was Santa Claus, but I never told. Each child received a little bag of netting filled with candy. It was sticky, since the candy did not have a wrapper on it in those days. It stuck together. We would eat the candy and an orange and an apple.

After the concert everyone walked home in the dark together. We would all be excited, waiting for Christmas Eve. This was a wonderful thing we did before Christmas.

The church stopped doing the pageant in the early 1940s. My kids went to Sunday school in the 1950s, but by the 1970s there weren't as many children, and they stopped Sunday School altogether.

Our Family Christmas

At home my dad would make the same kind of tissue paper Christmas garlands from each corner of our parlor with a bell in the middle.

We always had a big Christmas tree at our home. It was set up in the parlor, the front room where we had a piano. The tree was from the woods. Sometimes Daddy would cut two or three until he found the right one. My mother might think there was something wrong with it. Mostly spruce.

My aunts in Boston, Ella and Lorena, would send decorations every year. We had candle holders on the tree, and they were lit on Christmas Day. One time, my mother Elsie was lighting the candles and started at the bottom instead of the top. She lit the one on the bottom, stood on a chair to light the higher up one. The bottom of her dress caught on fire. A man visiting grabbed a mat and wrapped it around her dress to put out the flame.

For my first twelve years we would get dresses from my aunts in Boston. At the time, people got all their things from a catalogue, like Eaton's. As children we believed that the presents came from Santa Claus. I was probably seven or eight when I stopped believing.

On Christmas day we were allowed to go downstairs and get our stocking and take it upstairs with us when it was almost light. We had a little lamp on the hall floor that was lit at night.

After breakfast we washed up and got dressed, and then we could open our gifts. In my stocking, there was always an orange, maybe some grapes, candy and a small gift for my dolls, Santa Claus shaped soap, little things, and a new toothbrush. We always got money from our grandparents, 50 cents from my father's parents, and 25 cents from my mother's parents. Then we received another 50 cents at New Year's from my grandfather Grant. It had to be silver. We might get a total of a couple of dollars at Christmas. That was a lot of money then.

MILDRED GRANT. 1929.
MILDRED GRAY FAMILY
PHOTOGRAPH.
USED WITH PERMISSION.

At Christmas dinner we never had turkey. We had turnips, potatoes, carrots, never salad, but a big roast of pork with gravy. In later years we had goose with berries, especially cranberries. In much later years we started having turkey. Goose is very fatty. In fact, goose grease is good for open sores. My mother Elsie saved goose grease for a man up the road. He had something wrong with him, and he used it for healing.

On Christmas day, there was one church service. We could play in the snow, but there was no skating on Christmas. We could go to our friends' homes to see what they got. One year I got a teddy bear and an Eaton's beauty doll. Freda played with dolls more than I. She had a doll's bed and carriage.

Birds and Bees

When I was about 10, I wasn't very knowledgeable about the birds and the bees. For all Jean and I knew Grammy Reid's cat Martha's kittens came out of the ground. When I was young having a baby was having a secret. It was very private. People didn't talk about things like that then. Elsie and my Aunt Jemima would whisper about people in the family way. I think we knew what they were talking about, but we wouldn't say.

When my brother Kenneth was born I didn't know we were having a baby. Elsie had to have a C-section, and that was unusual. My sister was going to grade 12 in Sydney at the time, and I stayed with her while my mother was having Ken.

In those days, babies were mostly born at home. There was a doctor here at that time who would usually be at the birth. But it was never talked about, not at all. A maid staying with us told me a little bit about the "birds and the bees" when I was about twelve. One day, my friend's father saw me looking at an Eaton's catalogue picture of a baby carriage and said: "Wouldn't you like to be pushing one of those carriages"? I had absolutely no idea what he meant.

Any sexual stuff was totally secret. I was in school when I first got my period. I didn't know what happened. I told my mother, and she gave me stuff. There was no such things as supplies for that then. She told me "That happens to every girl." That was about it. Everyone was very private about sex life. It was all secret. Now they are teaching it in school!

Everything is out in the open now, even people's private lives. With a computer and someone's social insurance number you could find out everything about a person's history. Morse Code is probably the most private communication there is left, for those of us who understand it. There are things in life that should be a secret if you want it that way. Most people have some little thing that they don't want to reveal.

Young children see a lot now on TV especially, not just about having a baby. You can go on the computer and find out anything, and people's vocabulary is very crude. I have never gotten used to people using bad language. I really don't like it at all.

Recently I spoke with an old doctor whose boss at the hospital sent him out in a snowstorm to help deliver a baby. It was very hush hush, since the girl was not married, and the family didn't want anyone to know. The baby was born by the time he got there. He got stuck in the snow. But when he arrived he took the baby and the patient to the hospital. The girl's parents kept the baby. They were too poor to go anywhere. People whispered about it. It was an awful stigma to hold over a young person, both the mother and the baby. There was no birth control then. Now sex is too open. There is nothing left to the imagination!

Best Friends

I had two best friends when I was growing up, my cousin Jean Reid and my friend and neighbor Margaret MacDonald.

In the days before indoor plumbing, Grammy Grant called the toilet the "back house." One day, my friend Margaret and I made a cigarette out of Timothy grass and seeds. I don't remember if it was me or Margaret, but we stole a match from home. We went out to Grammy Grant's "back house" to try our cigarette. We thought we were in trouble when Grammy said "Someone's been smoking in my back house!" But I think she thought it was the maid or the maid's sister. Margaret and I didn't get caught.

Once we tipped over my cousins' outhouse, and we got in big trouble. This was at Halloween, and we were playing around. Within a month, people had electricity and running water and bathrooms. It changed everyone's life. Life changed so fast after that.

Margaret and I were together constantly our whole lives. She lived two doors away. When we were older, we each had a car and took turns going to cards and bingo games. I can hear her saying "There is not much snow on the road. There is one track. We can go." She was fearless about driving in bad weather.

Margaret was a year older than I, and we were friends until she died in 1990 at the age of 72. Margaret was very funny, and we always laughed and laughed when we were together. Margaret died suddenly shortly after Duncan did.

Just before she died, Margaret and I went to the traditional summer Strawberry Festival in Framboise. We stayed to clean up, so we left after others. We decided to go for a drive, so we went down on Canoe Lake Road. I was driving when the car got stuck in the mud. We were laughing. I put it this way and that way, and finally we got the car out. We were both outside trying to push the car out of the mud. But Margaret said she had a pain in her back. She thought it was gall bladder pain. We had been moving tables at the Strawberry Festival, and we thought that might have caused her gall bladder to act up.

The next morning, on Monday, Margaret had a seizure and was taken to the hospital. I went to see her, and she seemed to be doing fine. We were going to bingo on Thursday, and she thought she would be out of the hospital in time to go. But Margaret had a heart attack and died in the night. Lillian Harriss was the one who came to tell me that Margaret had died. It was August 23, 1990. Duncan had died on June 5th. Margaret's husband had died of cancer the previous November.

One shock right after another. Luckily I didn't take a nervous breakdown. We never get over such a heart-breaking shock. Margaret had two children. One lives next to me; one lives in Vancouver.

Up until recently my friend Hazel who also worked with me at the steel plant was the only childhood friend I had left. She lived in Sydney but we talked often and saw each other when she would come to Gabarus.

Ice Skating at Night

Winters were very different then. Lots of snow, and the ice stayed frozen harder and longer. We used to go ice skating at Harris Lake, named after the Dan Harris' family. There are three inlets at Harris Lake: first arm/lake, second arm/lake, third arm/lake. First arm is below the cemetery, the second arm was Roddy's field—his land jutted out into the lake, and the third arm was right next to Harris Beach.

When I was a teenager I got to go skating at night. My husband Duncan's father used to cut down big trees for a bonfire. I remember the sparks flying around in the night. And I can still remember the moonlight shining on the ice and the smell of burning spruce.

We used to make fudge in a big pot and pour it on the frozen lake. We used four or five bags of sugar and canned milk to make it. It was poured out in a square about three feet wide. Then the men would skate it into pieces.

So quiet. Ice was smooth, perfect. Girls would skate with their boyfriends. A few older people would be there like Duncan's father, a few people in their 50s. Usually, there were about twenty people or so, a lot of young people, teenagers 15-16, if you were allowed. But never on Sunday. Duncan's father was a wonderful skater himself, and he skated until he was well over 70. He was talented. He also played the concertina.

All the Grays were good skaters, and my children are good skaters too. Duncan's father and his daughters [Duncan's sisters] skated across Gabarus Bay to Kennington Cove and across the harbor in Sydney. Fred Reid, my mother Elsie's first cousin, was an excellent skater who could make a figure eight with his skates, and Alfred MacDonald, my friend from childhood, he was a terrific skater too.

The last time I skated I was about seventy. Duncan gave me new skates for Christmas, but my leg was still sore from a broken leg. Duncan helped me out of the car next to Little Lake but I couldn't skate. I took my skates off, and after I went home I packed them in a box and sent them to my daughter Karen. I cried. It was a real loss, because I had been a skater all my life. I had been skating since I was five years old when my first skates were "bob skates" with two runners on each skate.

Now, no one goes skating at night, and very few people go skating at all.

ICE BOAT, SECOND
LAKE GABARUS. 1942.
PHOTOGRAPHER UNKNOWN.
ITEM NUMBER 89-1216-
19424. BEATON INSTITUTE,
CAPE BRETON UNIVERSITY

Thrilling Ice Boat

A lot of people had ice boats, some for racing, and some for fun. Ice boats are sailboats on skates. Everyone built their own. There was a cross piece under the hull of the boat and skate runners on each side that piece. A rudder was on the back end, attached to the back skate, and that skate turned. The back skate controlled the steering. There was a handle to control the steering on the back rudder skate. The ice boat itself was fairly small, and they made it as light as possible. But they need to be strong too, especially if there were two or three riders. Most had at least two people in addition to the driver.

You would sit on the board with your feet up, kind of like a snow board. The driver, the person behind you, would steer with the skate rudder. The ice was like glass, smooth. Ice boats are so fast. It was thrilling to ride on an ice boat. There is nothing like flying along on the ice. It was so much fun. We would be yelling. I don't remember anyone ever getting hurt. Sometimes the boat would slide sideways in the wind. We would just fall off onto the ice, slide off onto the ice.

We used to go to Harris Lake below the [Lakeview] Cemetery. Harris Lake was the perfect place for ice boats. You need lots of wind for an ice boat. And there was a lot of wind there right off the ocean, at least 50 or 60 miles per hour. It is a big lake with several inlets bordering on the beach. We used to call the inlets "arms", first arm, second arm, third arm or first lake, second lake, third lake.

On a cold and sunny winter afternoon it was wonderful to be able to go so fast. We could go fast, like fury. Duncan's father's ice boat was a big one. It would hold 3-4 people. Grandma Gray used to sew the sail from flour bags. We sailed around the lake, going up the arms of Harris Lake almost a mile and then turn around and go out into the middle of the lake and up another arm. When I was young, we could never ever go on Sunday, on ice boats, skating or sledding, but in the end we used to go on Sunday.

There is ship building in the genes of people from Gabarus, and you could see that in the ice boats. Dan Harris, whose family owned Harris Lake and Harris Beach, had an ice boat until about five years ago. Sadly, Dan Harris died recently, but he was a great boat builder and could have built another beautiful ice boat, if he had wanted.

Gabarus-Louisbourg Ferry

Louisbourg was the nucleus of our area. For many years there was a ferry between Gabarus and Louisbourg. First the ferry was under sail. The Molly O'Toole was one of the first that I can remember. The Yafico was another ferry, I think engine powered. The Gabarus-Louisbourg ferry ran every day except in the winter until it ended in the 1940s after the war. Louisbourg was a center of banking and business for things you couldn't get in Gabarus. Quite a few people moved back and forth from Gabarus to Louisbourg, and Gabarus folks moved to Louisbourg in later years.

People from Gabarus both bought and sold things in Louisbourg. That is where they got their fishing supplies and where they went to take the train to Glace Bay or Sydney. After our doctor left Gabarus, there was a doctor in Louisbourg. In my mother's time they wrote their provincial examination in grade 9 or 10 in Louisbourg. I took my provincial exams in Grade 10 there.

Dan Harris' uncle was the captain of the ferry which came in and out at Government Wharf over by the lighthouse. It has been some time since Government Wharf has been used, but parts of it are still visible there now, west of the lighthouse. In my day we used to jump off the wharf. I remember jumping off when I was 16 years old. It was definitely in use then.

In 1936, the federal government also dredged the barachois to enlarge the access to the harbor in the area of the gut rocks. They used dynamite to blow up the rocks. The water would go way up in the air, and the children were all fascinated to see that.

The breakwater, Government Wharf, was rebuilt after a storm that same year. Unfortunately, the material wasn't good, and it deteriorated very quickly. I remember that my nephew from Sarnia, Ontario, visited in his homemade cement vessel in the late 70s or 80s, and he came in at the wharf at the breakwater. He built the boat himself and sailed it from Sarnia, he and another cousin of mine. Not long after that, the breakwater fell apart. A lot of people thought that it deteriorated because salt water sand had been used in the cement. Then the big storms wrecked it completely. Now all of the wharves are privately owned.

In the 1940s Gabarus was also very connected to Sydney and the train connections there. Until 1955 Cape Breton was an island accessible only by boat or plane. It was less than 1 mile from mainland Nova Scotia but really a world apart. When the causeway was completed, we were connected to Nova Scotia. Before the Causeway, you went to the mainland in the ferry from Port Hawkesbury. It took about 15 minutes. You could put your car on the train ferry. At that time, Truro was the center of train transportation.

GABARUS LIGHTHOUSE.
PHOTOGRAPH BY CLAIRE E.
SCHEUREN. 2012

Lighthouse and Landmarks

Fog comes into Gabarus very fast. It comes in quickly off of the ocean. We have a foghorn at the end of Rouse Island that the Coast Guard owns and takes care of still. Mariners always need all the help they can get. If the navigation systems fail, or if they don't have them on their boats, little boats especially may not know where they are. The lighthouse and the other landmarks are still important to fishermen and sailors. It is important to understand the old fashioned ways that people are used to and depend on, like the landmarks that they line up to get their bearings. When my father went out fishing he used to say: "the lighthouse sets the mark. I had the church in line with the lighthouse."

Swordfishing in the 1930s

Sword fishermen would follow the fish up the Atlantic Coast from Gloucester [Massachusetts]. Every summer there would be quite a few sword fishermen. They were very friendly young guys, and they made friends with the people in Gabarus.

The boats were special and the fishermen had to be very skilled. Like all fishermen, they had to be patient. Most of the boats were 30 feet and run by engines. At the front, they had a stand about 6 feet out. There was a board on top of the front of the boat with a railing around the end of it. That is where they would stand when they speared the fish. After the fish was speared, it would go crazy and try to swim away but the spear was connected to a rope and a lobster buoy. After the fish died, they would pull it in. They would follow it until the fish died. In those days, the swordfish were very big, 150-200 pounds. Sometimes a man with a dory would pick up the fish. It was a real skill to kill the swordfish with the spears. Now they catch it on trawls.

MILDRED GRANT ON JOHN GRAY'S SWORDFISHING BOAT. CA. 1939. MILDRED GRAY FAMILY PHOTOGRAPH. USED WITH PERMISSION.

Local fisherman would get up to three in a season. The Gloucester boats that came all the way up the coast to Gabarus and Glace Bay were mostly searching for swordfish. They would land at the breakwater and tie up their boats there (5 or 6 boats would be following the fish). They would go as far as Ingonish or Cape North. Mostly they were the same people every year. They were young men, in their twenties. They were really nice and always bought stuff at the local stores, including ice cream from our ice cream parlor which was a good place to go and hang out with the local girls they met. They stayed on their ships. They had girlfriends here, for sure. I was too young. They would bring girls into the ice cream parlor and sit around and talk for a long time.

Elsie Caught Wiley a Swordfish From the Window

Daddy had a license for swordfish, but he had never caught one. One Sunday Elsie was shaking her mats by the window in the kitchen. In those days, the big kitchen at our home faced the bay. Elsie saw a swordfish in the bay. Sure enough, Daddy went out and caught the swordfish. It was 185 pounds. We used to say "Elsie caught Wiley a swordfish from the window!" Now they are caught before they come into these waters or they catch little ones in trawls. At that time, my father speared it.

Lobster Factory

At one time, there was a lobster factory in Gull Cove and two in Gabarus. Each lobster factory probably employed about twenty-five people, mostly women with a few men who would do the cracking. Lobster was cooked and then canned. The women would be mostly washing and packing the cans. It was all done by hand. The cans were lined with a kind of wax paper before the lobster went in. All the workers had white caps and aprons. It had to be airtight on the can. I remember the man who sealed the cans. There was some kind of a sealing mechanism where he pressed his foot like on a treadle sewing machine, and it sealed the can airtight. Then they would put the cans in boiling water to check for the can being airtight. They were careful. They wouldn't sell it unless it was properly canned.

The first lobster factory in Gabarus, H.E. Baker's factory, was right on the barachois. The cook house for the lobster factory was behind it and is now a private home. I never saw that factory, since it was before my time, early 1900. Before that there was a lobster factory in Gull Cove. In the old days they would make their own tin cans from tin my grandfather and others brought in by boat. There were remnants of tin there for many years. We called it the tin pile.

Most of the lobster factories closed in the early 1900s. I think the last one closed around 40 years ago, in the early 1970s. The last lobster factory was over near the lighthouse.

Mostly people from here and the surrounding areas were the workers. I never worked in the factory, but my cousin Jean Reid did. Her job was washing lobster tails. That factory was the one over by the lighthouse. In the early 1940s probably. They would also make lobster paste of the roe and green part, grinding them together for sandwiches or a dip. We called it tomalley. I think you can still buy it. After it was blended, it was put in cans.

Fishing Changes in My Lifetime

Grandpa Captain Grant bought fish and cured it and shipped it to Halifax. Codfish was the main thing then. People also bought barrels of mackerel to send to Barbados, salt mackerel. It would be so many days in the salt.

A yaffle is a pile of salted codfish weighing about 15 pounds. They would take the yaffles and then spread them over the flakes to dry. In the summer, women would cure the codfish outdoors on flakes made of branches, formed into a big table. A flake is like a drying rack. It was made of wood, open, a frame, small sticks like dowels. The top would be saplings, just out of the woods. One side was open to lay the fish on. The frame was nailed 12 feet or 15 long, probably 4 feet off the ground. Men had already cleaned the fish and put it in a salt brine wash for a certain period of time. Then they would wash off the brine. Women would spread the codfish on the flakes and turn it over until it was completely dried out. They had to be separated out. They would put one fish down and then the other with the tail of the fish alternating. I think it took about two weeks to dry in good weather.

They would run to cover it if it rained. In those days there were no coyotes or wild foxes to sneak up and eat the drying fish. I think the foxes steered clear of people in those days. Now you can see a fox walking down the street at night. Some of the men did trap foxes at that time. They would carve out a rack and stretch the skins that my Grandpa Grant would buy and send them to Antigonish where I think they made them into neck collars on coats.

In my day people were interested in the economy. Everyone knew the price of lobster. It was 35 cents for large ones, and now it is around five dollars a pound. I think people are less interested in business, and there is a different customer service mentality. We really helped people who came into the store even if they didn't buy from us. In my day people were very accountable to each other.

People were interested in other people and did a lot of the same things, fishing and catching cod and curing them. Now there is a ban on catching codfish. To prevent overfishing, there are quotas on each fish now, and you are not allowed to catch codfish yet.

There have been a lot of changes to the fishing industry in my nine decades of life. Now there is a quota on crab, halibut, and they catch much smaller swordfish. There are fewer big fish like swordfish and tuna, although they still fish tuna around Gabarus and other parts of Cape Breton and Nova Scotia. Once my husband and his brother caught a tuna fish, but it was hard to sell, even for nine cents a pound. Now, if you have a license to fish for tuna, you can only get one, but that fish could sell for thousands to the Japanese. They ship it in ice right away from the Sydney airport, so it can get to Japan within the day.

The fishermen in Gabarus used to make nets out of lobster twine for their lobster traps. I used to help by cutting bows of young wood shaped in a circle and threading it through the netting. This made the entrance to the lobster trap. This was done into the 80s. Now they don't make their own. They don't use wood any more. Mostly lobster fishermen use wire traps from Prince Edward Island.

Everyone had their own mark for the buoys on their lobster traps. My grandfather Albert Reid had one that was all white with a red strip. Duncan's was all black with an orange strip around the middle. People would make up their own. No two were the same. They still do this, even though they are made of heavy plastic now.

A lot of equipment has been invented that has changed the fishing industry a lot, things like radar and fish finders. It is still hard work but not quite as dangerous. All boats now have to have life vests and flares and other safety equipment, and it is enforced. That is all new. Regulations did make fishing safer.

Summer of 16 Ice Cream Parlor

Over the summer when I was 16 I had an ice cream parlor in a building across from the family store. It was right next door to our home. I sold ice cream, bananas, and cigarettes. The ice cream parlor had a private room with a table where you could sit down and eat. I had bananas on the stalks. I actually sold lots of cigarettes and different ice cream dishes.

In those days parents wouldn't allow kids to smoke. I don't think there was a law that said you had to be a certain age. But in those days, you respected your parents, and you did what they said. They would keep you from doing anything illegal or bad. And they would punish you for getting in trouble. There were spankings, no such thing as "time out." You would not be able do some favorite thing. Kids listened to their parents more. My kids did, as far as I know! You expected to be punished if you got in trouble.

I charged 5 cents a cone and 15 cents for a sundae with syrup. I had three kinds: chocolate, pineapple, and strawberry. One bottle of syrup lasted a whole summer. My big sundae customers were the sword fishermen from Gloucester who used to come in at least three boats at a time, a lot of friendly young men.

I made $25 for two months work. That was a time when women started to wear pants, so I bought navy blue sailor pants, the kind with the button placket flap at the front. I bought them from Eaton's catalogue. It was the first time I had pants. They cost less than $5, so I still had $20 left. I thought I was rich!

Provincial Exams and Peroxide

In the summer of 1937 I took provincial exams in Grade 11. I had to travel to Sydney Academy to take the exams with students from all over Cape Breton. My good friend Albert MacDonald was there too. We were taking English A and B. My mother gave me a lot of instructions: "Be careful, you have heels on your shoes. You are not used to heels." I thought they were high heels, but they were what we called "Cuban heels" about an inch high, and my mother was worried that I would fall in front of a car!

The other girls weren't dressed up like I was, and I felt inferior to the other girls who kidded me about what I was wearing. They were from Sydney. I had all new clothes, but they were too fancy for school. We thought we needed our Sunday clothes for Sydney. Before that time, I had only been to Sydney on our outings once a year. When I was growing up we hardly ever went to Sydney, just the few trips with my mother and my Aunt Jemima, and the time I had to have my appendix out. Most of the time, we stayed in Gabarus or nearby.

In those days my hair was very blonde, white. I was a towhead. To take the exam I got all dressed up, but I think I still looked like I was from the country. In the exam room two particular girls sat near me, one in front and one behind me. They were clearly very good friends. They laughed and giggled and talked about me and passed notes, talking about peroxide bleach and making comments about me being from the country. They thought I dyed my hair! At that time, we had to write the exams in ink pen. Tears blotted my paper.

I didn't get my marks until the middle of summer, but I passed the test. But even before I knew the results of the exams, I was able to enroll in a two-year program at the business college in Sydney to learn how to type, do shorthand, business spelling and business writing.

Later, the two girls were in business college with me, and they became my good friends. They were ashamed that they made fun of me. We were in contact with each other until they died in their 80s.

I graduated in 1939. My first job was working for Sydney Motors in a filling station as a stenographer working the office, typing, and receptionist type tasks. I found that job by answering an ad. I worked there for a year, and then I got a job at the steel plant and I worked there for three years for Dominion Iron and Steel. When I worked at the steel plant, I was the private secretary to an auditor. I was good at shorthand which was used then. The auditors did all the books for the company. There were about 200 women working in the office. They were like accountants. In those days, the records were handwritten. There were no computers, and we used to add the old fashioned way. Later, in 1943, I went to work for the Sydney Ship Supply which supplied the military with the provisions to take to England for the war.

MILDRED GRANT GRAY.
CA. 1942. MILDRED GRAY
FAMILY PHOTOGRAPH.
USED WITH PERMISSION.

Pet Monkey

One of Daddy's friends was on a ship that went back and forth from Halifax to the West Indies. In the early 1940s, he sent a monkey to Daddy as a joke. The monkey arrived in a box on the mail truck. We fed him bananas and kept him in an empty room upstairs on the second floor of the store. We had him for a couple of years. He was quite tame, and we liked to play with him. He was never really house trained, and we finally had to give him away. He didn't have a name. We called him "monkey." My mother didn't care for it, and she was glad when we gave him away.

The Day Grandpa Captain Grant Died

Grandpa Captain Grant was living with us after Grammy Grant died in 1930. One afternoon, May 24th, 1939, he died suddenly. He was 81. My father was 81 when he died too. Grandpa Grant had come home to get some cash in the upstairs bedroom where he kept his cash box. He died just sitting on the bed. At the time, Elsie and another woman were wallpapering the kitchen. He had a heart attack and died right away.

I just loved that man. I was away when he died. It was the first time I was in Halifax. I remember the exact day because it was the Queen's birthday holiday, and I was celebrating it with my friend Hazel. Her father had a car, and they were visiting friends in Halifax. We stayed in a hotel all night. That was a first for me.

My grandfather Grant gave me many special gifts, including a calendar from a store up the road. I was three years old when he gave me the calendar picture of a little girl saying her prayers. I still treasure it.

Grandpa Captain Grant liked everyone, and everyone liked him. He was an emotional person, excited, enthusiastic, a very energetic kind. At that time Grandpa would feed people all winter from the store. Some people "forgot" and didn't pay, but he didn't care. He didn't get mad if people didn't pay, and when she was alive, Grammy Grant would go along with what he said. They were both good generous people.

Both Grandpa Grant and my father also helped people by employing them. They would give people necessities in the winter, and in the summer most people would pay with fish. When my Grandpa Grant died in 1939, my father took Grandpa Captain Grant's book of all of the unpaid bills and threw it in the stove. I can see the flame now. My father said "They didn't owe it to me!" Everyone started fresh.

Gloom Over the Community

I was in school in Sydney in the winter of 1940 when there was a terrible incident at Harris Lake one night around 6 or 7. Four kids, all in their teens, were skating arm in arm, and they went off the ice into the water. It was dark. They were on third lake next to the beach. Since that was the closest part of the lake to the beach, the ice was thin there. The salt water nearby makes the ice not freeze as well. The sea comes over there. They didn't see the hole in the ice. Laura, Theo (a girl named after her uncle Theodore), and Leticia were the three Gabarus kids. Leticia drowned, and Laura got out and was able to pull Theo out. A boy drowned too, a young man from Gabarus Lake. I think they were about 14 and 15 years old. Leticia was buried at Lakeview. Daddy was undertaker at the time.

Theo and Laura lived. But Theo was not destined to have a long life. In later years, Theo was living, married, and working in Halifax in a clothing store when fire broke out. She died of smoke inhalation. Laura got Alzheimer's young and lived until last year in Toronto.

The whole tragedy cast an awful gloom over the community.

World War II

During World War II we had blackouts because the Germans were off the coast. We had to cover the windows at night with special blackout blinds, but people weren't that scared. Those were the days before electricity, when we had oil lamps, so there wasn't a lot of light coming from the village anyway.

But there was a lot of concern about the war. I was in my early twenties at the time. When the war was on, I also had a job, a volunteer job, spotting enemy airplanes. I had a chart that showed the different types of planes. If I saw one from the chart, I called to report it. I only saw two that needed to be reported. It turned out there was no danger, not enemy planes. Mr. MacDonnell was in charge of that department at the time.

A lot of our boys went to war. Two friends of mine landed in Normandy with the Allied Forces, but they came back. They were among the first troops to land and wade ashore. The war was definitely felt here. One boy from here didn't survive the war. Bobby Martin was killed. He went to the Hill School, down the road from the Barachois School that I went to.

When the war was on we had ration cards for a certain amount of staples each month. Tea, sugar, and butter were rationed, and this was when we were first introduced to margarine. It came in a bag with a yellow color bubble to spread, kneading it to make it look like butter.

We ate what we had. I don't remember anyone complaining. People simply adjusted to the different circumstances. Older people in the village have lived through so many changes, all changes that have taken place, not just in my life.

When the war was on, I worked at a ship chandler, Sydney Ship Supply. I was working to help the convoys get ready to leave Sydney at midnight. They were all supply ships, for troops, and live animals like sheep and pigs and chickens and all kinds of equipment that they couldn't buy in England. Five or six men from Gabarus transported the supplies in small boats from the ship chandlers to the ships.

> **WARNING**
>
> **IT IS FORBIDDEN** to mention **SHIPS,** or **SHIP MOVEMENTS, AIRCRAFT, TROOPS, WAR INDUSTRIES** or the **WEATHER** during Long Distance Telephone Conversations.
>
> MARITIME TELEGRAPH & TELEPHONE CO., LTD.

WARTIME WARNING IN CAPE BRETON. CA. 1940. MILDRED GRAY FAMILY PHOTOGRAPH. USED WITH PERMISSION.

We shipped bonded liquor and cigarettes from the Sydney Ship Supply warehouses. There were two keys to open the bonded warehouse, one for the customs officer and one for the owner. The customs officer needed to be there when the door was open, so that he could monitor the bonded goods. I would make up the detailed manifest for the supplies of everything that went overseas.

Many of the supply ships made it home but others were torpedoed. A couple of the ships were torpedoed right off Sydney Harbour. Although the Germans sank ships close to Nova Scotia, they couldn't get into Sydney Harbor. During the war they had a steel net across Sydney Harbour, mostly to keep out submarines. The supply ships left in convoy during the night via different routes. They would open the net when the supply convoy left. We were always sad to see them leave. It was so uncertain how far they would get, if they would get home, or to the port they were going to. The supply ship men were strong-willed, and they didn't let on that they were worried about whether they would make it. Between weather and submarines, it was a very dangerous voyage in those days.

There were a lot of Greek ships helping with supplies. The *Pancheto* is one that I remember. A particular captain of a Greek ship asked me to buy a sewing machine for his wife, and I did. But he and his ship, and the sewing machine, were torpedoed near Newfoundland. As far as I know, everyone died.

When I first went to Sydney to work during the war, I lived in a rooming house and sometimes with my sister Freda. By that time, Freda was a registered nurse and worked at the hospital. Freda wore a starched white uniform to work every day. Now there is no distinction in uniforms. People have given up a lot of their identity. People are so casual now.

At the time, we had the steel plant, and there was good security. Iron ore to make the steel came from Wabana, Newfoundland. They made steel rails. During the war, some of the ships bringing the ore were torpedoed by German U-boats on their way to Sydney. The steel plant closed in the eighties. At the end, apparently, it wasn't good steel, and they couldn't sell their product. Not the type of steel needed in later years, and the railroads stopped needing the steel rails.

Between the 1940s and 1960s, there used to be a chain of suppliers for coal mining and the steel plant. A lot of people made their living that way. Then the mines and the steel plant closed. Now there is no industry in Sydney, only car dealers and the repair of cars. It happened fast, within 10 years after the steel plant. The closing down of coal and steel caused a shift in the workforce, since people had to leave Cape Breton to get jobs. When the steel plant was built in the early 1900s, there was a huge need for workers, so a lot of people came to Cape Breton from all over the world: Russia, Italy, Eastern Europe. After it closed, there was a huge drop in population.

BERYL MARKHAM'S PLANE. 1936. PHOTOGRAPHER UNKNOWN. ITEM NUMBER 89-1216-19390. BEATON INSTITUTE, CAPE BRETON UNIVERSITY.

Buzz and Beryl

Gabarus and the area had more than its share of contact with famous aviators too. Buzz Beurling was a famous fighter pilot and Second World War hero who landed his little plane on the beach in Gabarus. I think he was only 26 when he died. And Beryl Markham is another aviation pioneer who made history near Gabarus when she was the first woman to fly solo across the Atlantic from east to west in 1936. Her plane crash landed in Baleine Cove, just up the coast from Gabarus.

JACKIE GRAY WITH BUZZ BEURLING PLANE ON GABARUS BEACH. CA. 1946. MILDRED GRAY FAMILY PHOTOGRAPH.
USED WITH PERMISSION.

Wartime Wedding

Duncan and I were married on October 11, 1941. I was 21, and Duncan was 26. He was working in Sydney at the steel plant in the billet department, and I was a secretary at Dominion Coal. The war was on, and a lot of people were getting married. It was 1941. Everything was different during that time.

On Thursday, Duncan said "Let's get married on Saturday." We went to a minister in Whitney Pier who said that we needed a license. We had to hurry since it was Thursday. We got the license, got a ring, I bought a new dress and shoes, and we went to the church on Saturday.

The minister said: "Do you have witnesses?" We didn't. He said: "The lady next door may be able to help." And she came over with her apron on and signed the paper. After the wedding we went to supper and to stay for two nights at the Glace Bay Hotel. That was our honeymoon.

Other times we went to the Glace Bay Hotel too, especially in the winter when we couldn't get home. One time at the hotel I saw a man I knew from home and he said, "What are you doing here?" I told him that we were married, but that no one knew yet. I asked him not to tell, and as far as I know he never did. I knew this man because in 1929-1930 this man came to Grandpa and Daddy to see if there was some work. They gave him some work, and he stayed at Grammy's.

We didn't want anyone to know, since married women were not allowed to work. I couldn't have worked in my office if I was married. We were married in October, and we told our family in May on my birthday of the following year. Duncan and I were both boarding in separate houses, and we came to Gabarus almost every weekend.

It was important to us that we were married whether anyone knew it or not. I was married in October and Karen was born in July of the following year. I was married 9 months and 9 days when I had Karen. After Karen was born, I had to give up work.

MILDRED GRANT GRAY.
CA. 1942. MILDRED GRAY
FAMILY PHOTOGRAPH.
USED WITH PERMISSION.

Although the war was on, and they needed every able bodied person to work, in this particular steel company office they did not allow married women.

Finally, I had to tell my parents I was married. When my parents found out that I married Duncan, my father wrote me a letter, and so did my mother. Her letter was tough, concerned about what was we were going to live on. His letter said "Don't worry. Your mother will get over it." And she did. At first Elsie was mad because I was having a baby by the time we told her.

I had Karen in July 1942, and my mother wasn't entirely happy that I had married without her knowledge or blessing. Daddy accepted the fact that I had gotten married, but Elsie was not quite as accepting of the idea at first. It didn't take long for her to get used to the surprise. Elsie loved Duncan, and he was very kind to her, especially at the end of her life. Duncan was that type of person, very generous and supportive.

And when I left home they gave me a set of Spode china as a wedding present. By then I had to quit my job. There were two showers for me in the office: My co-workers gave me a bedroom chair, and there was a poem that went with that too: "Mildred is leaving us today and very soon she will turn Gray and leave her everlasting files to gladden Duncan with her smiles" was one verse of about ten.

DUNCAN AND MILDRED
GRAY AT 40TH WEDDING
ANNIVERSARY. 1981.
MILDRED GRAY FAMILY
PHOTOGRAPH.
USED WITH PERMISSION.

Duncan came from Gabarus too. Duncan and I grew up together. Duncan grew up with his seven brothers and sisters in the house where I live now. His father was a fisherman, and the family ran the post office for 45 years.

Duncan and I liked each other for all our lives. Duncan was a loveable person. He was 5' 8 ½, same as me. We really knew each other. We played together as children, and we were always friends, together all the time. I went with Duncan and then with other people. Courtship was certainly different then too. We went skating. We weren't allowed to do much else. There was a lot of visitation, couples visiting other couples, playing cards, spending time together at community events. Courtship was about being together, visits, playing games, going for walks and skating together. Twice a year there were silent movies using the projector here in the hall.

When Duncan and I first married we had a little house in Sydney, and had moved a couple of times. It wasn't a great situation. I got a different job, and hired a girl to look after Karen. She was still a baby, going on 2. So I was able to work for a season at the ship chandlery, Sydney Ship Supply.

Then Duncan got sick. We had nothing, so we came back to Gabarus and lived with his mother and father. His father died that first year. Mrs. Gray had the post office, and Duncan and I also did it for a year, but after the war, the job had to be awarded to a veteran, and Jim Allen got it. Also, we weren't allowed to have two government jobs in the family. So after I became the telegraph operator, Duncan had to quit. Then we went into the business of buying lobsters. This is the kind of work that he did until he died in 1990 at the age of 75.

We didn't have much, but we did OK. We did better for ten years before Duncan died. We got along good. Our marriage was not threatened by each other's interests. He did what he wanted and supported me in what I wanted. Neither of us was jealous or threatened by each other's interests. I think we were both generous people.

Duncan had a lot of sickness and pain in his life. When Duncan was 15 years old he had appendicitis. He was poisoned by the infection and got a bone marrow disease, osteomyelitis. He had many operations, bone surgery, two plates in his arm, and a few in his legs. He had trouble moving his right arm. He would never say there was anything wrong. He never complained.

Duncan was often in the hospital, and at that time we had to pay. It was very hard to pay those bills. In those days $4 a day was still a lot of money. We would get one bill paid, and then there would be another, and he had to take pain pills. They cost money too. It never went into his head or spine, but he limped after a few operations where he had had plates put in.

When he was older it came out and got much worse. For many years, Duncan was very sick with his osteomyelitis. One summer when I was going to Boston, Duncan had a lobster license, and he was putting his lobster traps out, but he couldn't haul them in. He was so sick. He had a slight limp mostly all his life. One year he went in hospital in May and came out on Armistice Day November 11th. It was so bad. Then a miracle happened.

One of our ministers in Gabarus was the seventh son of a seventh son; we believe they have the power to heal. He prayed for Duncan when his health was really bad and the doctors thought his leg should be amputated.

The minister came and had the children kneel down and pray. Shortly after, a doctor from Australia came to Sydney. He was an orthopedic specialist and surgeon. His opinion was that the leg did not need to be amputated. He wanted to try medication first. At the time, the medication was new. I remember the names of the medicines as dignan and linkenson. That doctor only stayed in Sydney for a short time, but while he was here he saved the day. I have always believed that the minister's prayers brought that doctor to us.

Duncan had suffered from the age of 15 to about 65. In the last ten years of his life he had no osteomyelitis. Duncan was good looking and always looked young for his age, and he was young in his ways. He had hardly any grey hair when he died at 75. Antibiotics were available by then, and he had good medical care to prevent osteomyelitis.

Although Duncan had a lot of health issues, he helped me out a lot. At night, he would take over the switchboard, so I could get a little sleep.

Lobster Buyer Business

Lobster has always been a big part of the commerce here. Duncan went into the lobster business starting in the late 40s and 1950s. We would supply fisherman with some equipment (paint, ropes, lath for the traps, etc.). When Duncan made up their payment, we would deduct those expenses. So the lobster fishermen didn't have to borrow money from a bank or a credit union. They didn't have a coop movement here. All the lobster buyers supplied the fishermen. It was all the same method. It was worth it for the fisherman and the buyer. In the 1980s, when there were at least 25 boats fishing out of Gabarus, there was more than one buyer, but we bought more than half.

A lobster fisherman could make enough money in two months of lobster season to last the whole year. During the season, we used to pay every two weeks. We paid in cash. We never owed money and had always been able to meet demands.

In 1948, we bought lobster from 32 boats, in the 1980s from about 25. Now there are only 9 boats fishing lobster. In the early days of our business, the live lobsters were iced and shipped to the States in crates by truck. Some people were shipping lobsters to the Boston fish pier, since there were three or four buyers in Boston. Dench and Hardy was one of the companies they shipped them to in Boston. I have seen the lobster crates from Gabarus on the Boston wharf. At that time, Gabarus fishermen got more than if they sold them locally. Now lobsters are shipped by refrigerator trucks and by airplane.

In the 1980s a truck would come and take the lobsters to PEI to a canning factory. The price was low at that time. It was about 53 cents a pound for large lobsters. It was less for small lobsters called "canners." There is a metal tool that measures the size from the eye to the end of the body. That is how it was determined which kind of lobster it was and whether it was a legal length. "Market" lobster was above the 4" measure that went from below eye socket to the end of the body. Small lobsters were called "shack", and they were to be canned. You have to throw the very small ones back.

Selling The Store

In 1950, my father fell off the roof of the Grant Store. He was making it into one story and repairing the roof. That's when he fell off. He hurt himself badly, especially his back and legs. We knew he was in pain, but he didn't complain. Daddy was never the same after.

We sold the store in 1954, but the store still ran for more than 20 years after, until around 1975. Daddy was 72 when he sold the store. He was still Justice of the Peace, but he was not an undertaker anymore. The last calendar of the Grant Store was for 1954. The calendar was sponsored by Robin Hood Flour, a Canadian company, I think it is a Winnipeg company.

My father sold the store, because he found out that he had cancer, and he wasn't well for the next ten years before he died in 1965 at the age of 81. His illness didn't keep him from doing anything he wanted to do until the last little while.

By the mid-1950s, people were starting to buy things in Sydney, and over the next thirty years there were gradually fewer and fewer stores. John MacGillivary bought the store from my father, and then Dan and Alice MacDonald ran it for over twenty years into the late 1970s. Dan had a van and used to go to Sydney every Thursday for supplies. Gerry and Earl Sherwood owned it, the MacLeods were the last owners. They sold it to Raymond Sutherland. The old Grant Store finally closed in the 1980s, and the Sutherlands tore the building down.

There were a few other stores in the 1980s, perhaps four or five including a store down by the hall. More and more people had cars. Gabarus stores lost business. By then people were buying most of their groceries in Sydney. The last store in Gabarus was owned by Annie and Charlie Hardy. It was outside the village, right next to the old Hill School.

Even if there was a grocery store in Gabarus now, I think that people would go into town. People are used to it now.

After Daddy sold the store, most people were dying in hospital, so Daddy also moved the other building where he used to keep the caskets and where I had an ice cream parlor in 1936. He sold it to a man who made a house out of it. In those days a lot of houses were moved around and pieces built on them. Now that house has been moved across from where I live now, and it belongs to Gerry and Earl Sherwood, and they built a piece on it. The bones of the house are still there, even though it was moved around a lot. A lot of history.

Living History

The houses in the village are living history. All the old houses were made of wood that came from here, the original wood. One man, I think his name was Hector MacKinnon, built a lot of houses in Gabarus in the late 1800s, salt boxes, just a square house. The home where I grew up was built by him in 1912.

Around the same time there was a traveling artist named Thorneycroft who came to the village. He painted ceilings with different scenes, like trees. Dan and Diane Harris had one, and at Dale Hardy's there is a painting on the ceiling that was painted around 1910-12. Quite a few people hired the artist to do ceiling painting. There was lots of beautiful wallpaper too. Up to about fifty years ago everyone had wallpaper. Another man did hand painting in our house on the wall as you were going upstairs. On the wall we had roses and green leaves the whole length of the wall with a border along the ceiling. Many houses had that decoration.

The population of Gabarus has changed a lot over the last one hundred years or so, from around 1,000 in 1900, probably 500 when I was born in 1920, and now with about one hundred people living here and only about seventy during the winter. There are only about half the number of houses now. Over the years some houses were demolished. Many have been moved, remodeled, and some rebuilt. Of the houses today, almost all are over one hundred years old.

ONE WOMAN 911

REV. EWAN MACKILLOP AND CHRISTINA GRANT MACKILLOP. CA. 1936. MILDRED GRAY FAMILY PHOTOGRAPH.
USED WITH PERMISSION.

Christina Grant and the History of Morse Code in Gabarus

The history of Morse Code started in Gabarus in 1902 when a woman from Gabarus named Christina Grant was boarding at the home of Fletcher Townsend, who worked at the Louisbourg railroad station. His sister was married to a great uncle of mine.

The train went to and from Louisbourg to Glace Bay and to Sydney. They used Morse Code for the changing of the tracks. He said: "Why don't you learn the Morse Code, and you can get a job in Gabarus?" And she did. After she was trained in Morse Code in Louisbourg, Christina Grant lived with my grandmother in Gabarus. My grandfather Captain John Grant was her uncle. Her father was Absolom Grant, my grandfather John Grant's brother.

Christina Grant was the first telegraph operator in Gabarus, from 1902 to 1946. For a while, in the very early days, she worked in the telegraph office upstairs in the Grant Store, until my mother Elsie started the ice cream parlor. Then they moved it across the street to an old house where Christina was living and taking care of her grandmother. It was her grandmother's house, right across the lane from where I live now. That is where Christina Grant lived with the telegraph office in the home.

Christina was very private with the telegrams. Sometimes she would pass along some information that people would not have received otherwise like news about current events, not personal telegrams, but news of the outside world. Christina Grant was very responsible, but she was also a boisterous, fun loving, lovely person. Very helpful.

When she was about fifty years old, she married our widowed minister, Rev. Ewan MacKillop, and lived at Gabarus Lake in the manse. The telegraph office key was also there, so she would always hear if anyone was calling. She helped our minister raise his children after his wife died.

How I Became the Morse Code Operator

Christina Grant MacKillop was the operator for forty-five years until July of 1946 when she became ill with cancer and died not that long after. She was probably in her seventies at the time. Another woman with the same last name, Mrs. MacKillop, took her place. It was supposed to be a temporary job, since she had a big family in Grand River. She brought two of her daughters to go to school in Gabarus and planned to stay for six months. I thought she would stay longer.

I was invited by Mrs. MacKillop to take the course on Morse Code. It was a good government job, and I started to learn it in November of 1946. At the time I was pregnant with Albert, and I could do my training by simply walking to the telegraph office across from my home on Memory Lane. I was taking my time, since there was no sense of urgency.

All of a sudden that changed. One day in March 1947 Mrs. MacKillop had a pain in her heart. She called her son Kyle to take her to the hospital, and she died at 9 p.m. that very night. Immediately, I received a call from an official at the Federal Department of Transportation, now Fisheries and Oceans, who asked me: "Do you think you can do it? There are four night letters [which have forty words in each]; two of them are in French." I said: "I'll try!" I had to stay up all night and struggled with the French. It was a trial by fire.

In those days, telegrams were written with an ink pen. My tears blotched the words, and it was hard to make out what I had written. I was scared to death. I said to myself "You have to get over this!" I thought about the Grant family motto: "Keep strong." I asked God to help me, and he did.

All things happen with a purpose; we may not understand right away, or ever. Anything you have to do, you can do it! Nothing is impossible.

Later I had to take an exam to get Morse Code licensure. The test was very practical. A man in North Sydney had to make sure I knew the Code. He would send me a message, and I answered back, showing that I understood and could respond correctly. I took it just before the government entrusted me with the Morse Code key. At that time there was no pension for the position, but you had to be in the civil service to have the job.

When I became the telegraph operator, I had to take an oath of confidentiality. I took an oath promising not to tell any thing I learned or heard. I was not allowed to tell anything people didn't know. I couldn't tell anything, even if the doctor was out and someone had a baby. If anyone asked me for information, I would tell them that I wasn't allowed to talk about it.

Yes, it's true. I was the center of all the information. I knew what was happening with everyone. That was a lot of responsibility, and emotionally it was sometimes hard. From the time they entrusted me with that key, I felt very responsible. I always did. It all had to go through me---Gabarus Central. I was on 24-hour duty. If I was awake I could hear it easily, and I could hear the relay from bed.

Gabarus Telegraph Office

From 1947-1959 I was responsible for the telegraph central office in Gabarus. I would take a message in Morse Code and deliver it by hand or call and repeat it in English for 18 stations through communicating with my community contacts in Main-à-Dieu [pronounced in Cape Breton: "Manadew"], Framboise, Fourchu, Bateston, Baleine, L'Ardoise [pronounced in Cape Breton: "Lordways"], and other communities along the eastern shore. There were very few phones before the switchboard. We did have one because of the store.

Until 1962 when the telegraph office was closed by the federal agency, my whole life was tuned in to the click of the Morse Code key. GU in Morse Code were my call letters. G is "--. (dash dash dot)", and U is "..-" (dot dot dash).

The Morse code telegraph key and relay was connected with dry cell batteries at first and later electricity. Before me, the operator had to make the batteries by hand from mercury and lime. I was able to use B batteries before we had electricity.

You tapped the key in Morse Code to send a message. You would hear the message the same way, in tapping that communicated the letters. I would receive the messages in Morse Code and translate them into English or some French. I could understand both Land Code and International Code. Morse Code is no longer used in the Canadian Navy. It was eliminated about four years ago, but you still need to know 13 words of Morse Code to get a ham radio license.

In Morse Code one dot makes a big difference. The numbers make a difference too, and you must have the date right. In those days, telegrams were handwritten in ink on green paper. I spread the word via telephone and people carried the messages by foot, door–to–door.

I learned Morse Code like a language. I could take Morse Code in French and English including all letters and punctuation. Sometimes you know where the word is going by the first letters: quality, quick, queer. You can track on the meaning of the word.

Before Morse Code communication was so slow, mostly by letters. At the time, virtually no one had phones, and after letters sent through the mail, telegrams were the main way people communicated, especially in emergencies. I would get a lot of telegrams, especially on weekends. On Monday I would get forty-word night letters. I had to acknowledge each one: OK and at the end type "STOP."

Gabarus was the central telegraph. Mounties would come to my office. If there was a disaster this was the center of communication. I would relay messages from here. If there was shipwreck or other disaster I would find out who to contact and where to send the message, especially if it was a death notice.

I covered a big territory, right up to L'Ardoise. There was another telegraph office in L'Ardoise which closed down right after the hard rock mine in Stirling closed. That mine was owned by a Montreal company, so I used to have to take their Morse Code messages in French and translate them into English. I had taken French in grade 11 and wasn't totally fluent, but you get used to the contents of the telegram. For example, they were mostly about mining, and I got used to those words. To be sure, I would look some up. And I worried about missing a number or getting it wrong. That never happened. I worked hard. I was careful, but I was lucky too.

Each of these small communities around Gabarus had a local person who would deliver the telegrams. There were some with whom I worked more closely than others. In Main-à-Dieu, Mrs. Lathigee would deliver the telegrams after I called her with the message. Like the other government telegraph couriers who were paid by the Federal Department of Transportation, she was one of the few people with a telephone. In a typical day there could be nine or ten telegrams depending on businesses. She applied for the job. Mrs. Lathigee lived in a house with her husband Tom and twelve children.

The Gabarus Telegraph Office was at the center of everything that was going on: hospitals, doctors, babies, shipwrecks, death. I acted as a go-between with doctors and the RCMP. Mounties from Glace Bay covered the Gabarus area. I had to call the Mounties from time to time, but mostly I had to call doctors.

At first I was always sad and crying for someone else's troubles. Telegraphs were for special occasions, mostly troubles. Sometimes I would be crying before I got to the place to deliver the bad message. I am so softhearted. I had to call doctors all the time to make house calls when people were sick or having babies. In those days, there were very few accidents that people couldn't handle.

I had to deliver so much bad news. It was heart breaking for me, as well as the people to whom I delivered the messages. Telegrams were usually bad news, and people would be afraid if they saw me coming, especially if anything was going on in their family. My husband, Duncan, too, since he would help deliver telegrams. If it was not bad news, I would sometimes shout out "It's OK. It's not bad news!" as I approached.

Fortunately there were good messages too, people just staying in touch, checking in with their families. There were two men whose wives were living here. The men were working on the Great Lakes, and they were always sending messages to their wives like "On our way home!"

PHOTOGRAPH OF MILDRED GRAY IN 1948 AND MORSE CODE KEY. FROM ARTICLE IN HALIFAX CHRONICLE HERALD, OCTOBER 31, 2005. ARTICLE AND PHOTOS BY JOCELYN BETHUNE. USED WITH PERMISSION.

Telegrams and Bad News

One day Duncan delivered a telegram to a woman to tell her that her brother in St. Peters had died. She had the screen door locked. Duncan said he had bad news, and she fainted on the inside of the door. Duncan didn't know what to do. Fortunately, her husband arrived home from the grocery store right then, and he pushed in the door.

Another time I went to tell a lady that her husband had died. She was on her hands and knees and just looked up and said "The old rascal should have died long ago!" and she kept on scrubbing the floor. I can see her now, scrubbing the floor.

After the telegraph office was moved here to my house, a family rented the old house across the street, a poor family. They had five kids and very little money. They would come over to borrow sugar or tea.

One day the youngest girl ran over and said "Come quick. The baby is dead!" Albert was at home, and we both went right over. A three or four week baby who died of crib death was on the table. Albert took the woman and baby to the hospital. Very sad.

I saw a lot of tragedy. One day I had to deliver a telegram to a dying woman. She had untreatable cancer. When I arrived with the telegram, she was lying on the couch with her four little children playing under the table. I had to tell her that her husband in the sanatorium had just died of TB.

Shortly after that she herself died. Sadly the three-year old had TB like her father and only lived two or three months after the mother died. In her casket, the child looked like a sleeping angel. At the time, she was the same age as my daughter. The rest of the children were raised by her twin sister and did very well in life.

If I had lived in a city I would never have seen a lot of the life and death events that I did. Today, the mother would probably be in a hospice or hospital, and her children would be nowhere around. It was still a tragic loss, but the children were near their mother pretty much until the end. Maybe it was less of a trauma that way. I don't know.

Doctor and Vet Calls

When I was working on the telegraph, I would often call the doctor, and he would tell me what to do. In the 1950s, I had a call about a young couple from Newfoundland who were working way up in a wood camp. She was very young, and she was going to have a baby. The young man, only seventeen, and the sixteen-year old woman walked out to a house where a woman lived who had a phone to call me. The woman there told me to get the ambulance there right away. Luckily the woman must have had some training or experience as a practical nurse. The baby couldn't wait for the ambulance, so the woman helped deliver the baby. Then she sterilized the knife over the fire of the oil lamp, so she could use it to cut the cord. They stayed on the phone the whole time. The ambulance arrived after the baby was born, and the young mother and her baby both got in and rode to the hospital.

1950s Cow Gone Wild

One day when I was on the switchboard I had an urgent call for a vet. Two farmers who lived on the North Shore of Gabarus Bay, on the Louisbourg Road that is not open now, had a sick cow. They said that their cow was going wild, and that they had locked her in the barn. The cow was going crazy trying to get out. It was ready to have a calf, so they were very frightened, since the cow was so anxious to get out. I tried to call the vet, but at first I accidentally called the wrong number, and the man I talked to about a cow going wild must have thought I was a little nutty. But the man told me the name of the vet, and I was able to contact him and get him to come out. The vet tried to tell me what to tell them to do, but he said he would come out. It took him at least 45 minutes to get here. The cow didn't have distemper or some terrible problem. She had already had the calf, and she was trying to get back out to the barrens to be with her baby. That vet laughed and laughed.

Shipwrecks and Salvation

Some of my most harrowing memories were of shipwrecks that happened near Gabarus. As the Morse Code operator and later the switchboard operator, I was responsible for notifying the authorities and helping with the death notices to the families. For me, this was a difficult job. It was hard for me to prevent having an overwhelming emotional reaction to news about death and difficulty. Can you imagine what it feels like to be told that your loved ones died in a place you never heard of in your life?

Often I saw my own tears blotch the telegram paper. I am just as tenderhearted today. That is my basic nature. Yes, shipwrecks were especially heartbreaking. Living by the sea, it was sadly a common occurrence. You probably know that fishing is the most dangerous profession in the world. This is still true even though there have been so many changes in my lifetime from the days when my sea captain grandfather used the stars and a sextant to navigate.

So many technological advancements in navigation equipment, radar, GPS and safety requirements. Now the province checks to make sure boats have all the required safety equipment like life vests. When I was growing up, there was little attention or enforcement of safety. Not sure if the seas are safer now. When people make their living out on the sea, people expect hardships. A tragic death by drowning was an unspoken and constant worry for people like us who live by the sea.

The Wreck of the Marshall Frank in 1949

I have very vivid memories of the shipwreck of the *Marshall Frank*. Early in the morning of February 16, 1949, the *Marshall Frank* went right up on the gut rocks in nearby Framboise Cove. The *Marshall Frank* was one of the last of the two-masted fishing schooners, the same model as the *Bluenose*, like the kind my grandfather Captain Grant used to sail. Even though the weather wasn't bad, the boat hit a reef, and it was torn up. Five men drowned, and the others abandoned ship in life rafts. The men who drowned refused to leave the ship. They thought they would have a better chance if they stayed. The captain was saved. They interviewed him at my home.

The vessel was from Newfoundland, and I had to let the family know about the deaths. One man from Rencontre, Newfoundland had seven children. There was no road to where they lived; you could only get there by boat. Even the telegram about the deaths had to make a difficult trip, relayed along the telegraph offices across the other outports. It broke my heart to think of so many little children growing up without their father. Most fishermen only earned $200-300 a year in those days. So I was worried about the little children, and every year at Christmas I sent them mittens, hats and scarves that I had knitted.

SHIPWRECK OF MARSHALL FRANK. FEBRUARY 18, 1949. PHOTO BY VINCE RILEY. FROM CAPE BRETON POST.

But that is not the end of the story. A couple of years ago, Fraser MacDonald, a neighbor in Gabarus, traveled by boat to Rencontre. He was next to his boat at the wharf when a man said, "I see you are from Gabarus. Do you know Mildred Gray? Many years ago she sent mittens to my brother's children after he drowned in a shipwreck near Gabarus."

SHIPWRECK OF ICELAND II IN FOURCHU. FEBRUARY 26, 1967 PHOTO BY JOHN ABBASS, USED WITH PERMISSION OF BLAISE ABBASS FROM ABBASS STUDIOS.

Iceland II Goes Aground in Fourchu

Fourchu is one of the worst harbors in a gale. On February 25, 1967, there was a big southeaster snowstorm with high winds. The storm caused the wreck of the *Iceland II*, and nine men drowned. Many of the bodies were not recovered, although they found parts. Until a few years ago, part of the ship was still visible where it went aground on the rocks. It was a big steel-hulled boat. Some of the crew came from North Sydney. All the men died, because they were in the living quarters in the bottom of the ship, and they couldn't get out.

Interview with Spray Paint

In 1961 we changed over from Morse Code to Maritime Tel and Tel, to the switchboard. I had to be interviewed for the job, and the interviewers were coming to my home. At the time, we had open stairs painted green. When the two men arrived, I was spray painting the edges to make it look nice. I wanted to make a good impression. I had never used spray paint before. It wasn't spraying, so I put a nail hole in the can, and it started spraying green paint all over. I heard a knock at the door. I couldn't stop the paint spray, so I put the can under my dress! Later I had to use turpentine to clean it all up. It was a mess. But I kept my cool and was interviewed for the job, although they must have thought I was crazy. I got it. Those two men became my friends, and we always laughed about it. I had to throw away my skirt.

The Start of the Switchboard

MANUAL SWITCHBOARD CONSOLE CA. MID 60S. MILDRED GRAY FAMILY PHOTOGRAPH. USED WITH PERMISSION.

So I went to work for Maritime Tel and Tel running the switchboard for about another 15 years.

At that time there were about two hundred homes connected to me in Gabarus, Fourchu, Framboise, Stirling, French Road and past Framboise too. They would ring the phone by hand on a crank. The little disk here on my switchboard would drop down, and I would plug in a cord and talk, and push the little disk up. I had a headset, so I could hear. At one point, I hired girls to help with the switchboard, but it stayed in the room in my house: Angela, Susan, Shirley, Donna, and Marion. Some worked for me for five years.

It was a 24-hour a day job, just like the telegraph. But there were more calls than on the telegraph. People would call me anytime night or day. It was the same when I was on the telegraph. I would often get a call at 2 a.m. like "John has a pain. Call the doctor!" or "Call an ambulance!" "John is in a turn." The deaths and sicknesses were especially hard for me. I knew the people, and if people saw an ambulance they would call me to see what was going on.

Most were on four-party lines in Framboise and Fourchu. Many in Gabarus could afford one party lines. A lot of people were upset with the four-party lines, since everyone could hear what they were talking about if they lifted the receiver. It was good for me. When everyone had phones, I got out of the business of delivering bad news. They could talk between themselves, and I wouldn't know.

156 Bringing Out the Untold Life

Switchboard and Social Service

My family background helped me in my work too, since my work as a telegraph and switchboard operator was partially like social services work. I was able to help others. When I saw a family that had nothing, I was able to organize the boys who worked for me, the lineman and repair guys, to get gifts for them for Christmas. That was part of my calling that I was privileged and equipped to be able to do. Little things. A boy who had a birthday, and I was able to leave a pot of fudge on his doorstep. He is sixty now, and he has never forgotten.

I was fortunate to be a significant person in people's lives. People knew and trusted me. That made me feel even more responsible. I felt close to people. I felt so responsible for my job and for the other switchboard operators. I was a big part of people's lives, and they would want to keep in touch with me. There is nothing special about me, but I knew what people were going through. I was in a position to see. Many a potato I laid out on the doorstep [food when I knew they needed it]. One family always sends me a birthday card, since my birthday is near to their father's. Although I was the telephone operator, they all brought their babies to show me. I play cards right now with someone I helped have her baby.

People would call me night and day. I knew everyone's voice and number. I was memorizing numbers all the time. Since I covered the switchboard 24 hours a day, 7 days a week, I spent most of my life sleeping on my arm, especially in the summer when there were a lot of night calls. Quite often my husband Duncan would help out and handle the switchboard at night. Later I had other girls to help, two or three working shifts. Fortunately, I have never had a problem sleeping when I could. Even today, as soon as I put my head on the pillow, I am asleep. But if I need to wake up, I can do that quickly too.

People would call at all hours of the night to see about the weather, calling at 3 a.m. before they went out fishing. Or just for fun in the middle of the night. I always answered the phone, no matter what. I was always on call. I had a night alarm on the stairs, so I would never miss a call.

On the switchboard sometimes there would be five-six calls at the same time with one hundred people or more on the exchange. Very busy. People would also pay the phone bill at the switchboard office at my home, so there was always a lot of activity at the house.

Dying Family Friend

Some of the calls were harder than others. One night a man called and said "Middie, I am sick. I have a pain. Please call the ambulance. I think I am going to die!" I knew he lived alone and that he was around 80 years old. He was born about the same time as my father. This was about 1972. I called the ambulance to go to him. He lived near where the old church used to be.

I had known him since I was a little girl. He and his wife were good friends of my parents. Daddy and Elsie would spend the evening with him and his wife and play cards, and I would go along when I was little. He and his wife had a cat who slept under a newspaper on the floor. I loved to play with their cat. I would fall asleep while they played cards until 11 or so. They played auction 45. It is a bidding game. My father would tell jokes, and they would laugh. I know that his wife was born in Gull Cove. His wife had died of cancer, and they never had any children.

The bosses from the lobster factory used to stay at his house. I think he was a fisherman. There used to be an old age pension, and people would save money. It wasn't much, but they didn't need much. They would have their own meat for the winter. Most people had pigs, chickens and were rather self-sufficient. He was a nice man and a good friend to my family.

After I called the ambulance I stayed on the line with him. I said "Hold on --- the ambulance is coming." I knew it took thirty-seven minutes for an ambulance to get to Gabarus. But he said, "It is getting worse. I can't hold on, Middie. I can't hold on." Finally, I could see the ambulance company coming over Irish Brook and down Armstrong's Hill. In those days there weren't as many trees as there are now. I told him "I can see the lights of the ambulance coming down Armstrong's Hill! They'll soon be here." He said, "I don't think I can wait. I don't think I can wait." The phone went quiet. He died when we were on the phone together. At least he didn't die alone.

Two Young Lives Lost

In the later years of switchboard, around 1972-73, two young friends came to visit me one night. One was Billy Peters who was 20 and lived up the road. He was in art school in Halifax and had been in France. He had just gotten back and came to see me that evening. The other young man was Gilbert MacDonald who lived two houses from me. He was 18. His father and I grew up together. Billy and Gilbert and their friends were visiting that night, too many for the numbers of chairs we had, so they sat on the floor. The boys left my home around 10 p.m. At 3 a.m. I was called on the phone by the Mounties. There was an accident. The two boys had died in a car accident. It happened in Marion Bridge when a car came out of a blind driveway and hit them.

Destiny Calls

I crossed paths with a lot of people, some more than once. One day I was going to Sydney, and I picked up a hitchhiker. That was a common thing to do in those days, about 40 years ago. The young man said he had a baby and that he lived on French Road. He said: "We live in what was the duck house. We fixed it up." He said they didn't have many clothes for the baby. I don't think he and the mother were married. I came home, and spent all day Sunday making baby clothes. I had some nice flannel, and I made little night dresses and blankets. Duncan and I took the baby things over later that afternoon, but no one was home. We left the clothes there.

A month later, I was driving to Sydney again, and we saw the same young man lying by the side of the road. He looked like he was drunk or sick, but he was not near houses or anything. A couple of cars passed him, but we turned around. When we turned back we saw that he was bleeding profusely from a wound on his leg. He was as white as could be, lying on the ground and holding onto his leg. We managed to get him into the car and took him to the hospital. He had lost a lot of blood. But his clothes were so sticky with balsam sap; I think that actually saved his life. In the car I held his sticky clothes over the gash in his leg. It took forty-three stitches to clean it up. We found out that he had been in the woods cutting down a tree, and the saw fell on his leg.

Later I ran into him at Woolworth's, and he thanked me for my help and gave me a big hug. He told me that they had moved to Campbelldale Road and lived in a trailer, now with two babies. One night a few months later, someone called me to get the fire department and the Mounties for a fire on Campbelldale Road. This same man and his two babies died in the fire. At the time, the mother was out. The inspector told me why he couldn't get out. The trailer caught fire from the stove, and the fire was between where he was in the rocking chair and the door. He lost his life and his two babies.

MILDRED GRAY AND MARITIME TEL AND TEL EXECUTIVE AT RETIREMENT PARTY. DECEMBER 1976. MILDRED GRAY FAMILY PHOTOGRAPH. USED WITH PERMISSION.

Reluctant Retirement

December 21, 1976 was the date I retired. Up until then, my whole life had revolved around hard work. Aunt Ella died in 1976 on Halloween, and then on December 18, 1976 they closed the switchboard office. Dial phones were introduced. Gabarus was the last community in Nova Scotia to go on dial. It was a big year for me. Everyone had phones then. The time had come. I was the last manual switchboard operator. I was devastated, since I was so used to talking with people. It was quite upsetting. I was still young and in good health. The system simply changed.

When I returned everyone was asking me, "What are you going to do"? Even though I was just the operator there was a lot more to it. To me, it showed how they felt connected to me. They would tell me personal troubles or their happy days. I always knew about the tragedy first.

I still miss it. I was only 56. If you retire you should have something to take its place. I didn't want to retire. I had to. Hard to understand people not being interested in their work and not interested in learning every day. Competence is so rewarding. I miss my work terrible over these past thirty years.

Both times, when I went off the telegraph and then the switchboard, I think I had a little bit of an identity crisis. I didn't know what I was going to do. Who will I call?

At that time, I didn't really know how to drive. Before my retirement I only had Sundays to do anything. I decided to take driving lessons!

My kids were grown, and I had the means to travel thanks to Aunt Ella's bequest. So I was well over 50 when I did most of my traveling. That was the beginning of the next chapter of my life.

FAMILY AND THE FUTURE

Family Picnics

DUNCAN GRAY ON THE "GRASSY ROAD." 1941.
MILDRED GRAY FAMILY
PHOTOGRAPH
USED WITH PERMISSION.

Of course, some people thought that picnics were a waste of time, but Duncan and the children and I were happy for occasions when we could all be together. We would go on a picnic almost every Sunday. After dinner we would head out for a picnic. We didn't go very far, sometimes to Mira Gut, in a field, or by the water somewhere. If it rained we would sit in the car and have our lunch. At the time I remember we had a Plymouth. Telegraph messages were saved when I was gone. Our picnics were plain and simple. Tablecloth on the ground, with sandwiches, fruit and something to drink. I look at the basket now, and I almost cry, remembering.

We were a real picnic-going family. Even before we got a car we would take a basket to Gull Cove or Second Lake Beach. In those days we would take the grassy road on foot. This was the same place where we had a Sunday school picnic when I was a child. It was a great place for a picnic. It was right next to the lake with nice trees, a breeze, and a view of the ocean. When I was nineteen Duncan cut a heart and put our names in a tree there.

One day we were picnicking at a nice little place in Port Morien. We got all the stuff, and we were all set, and Duncan sat down right on an ants' nest! The children thought that was very funny. We all did.

The Sunday before Duncan died, he and I went on a picnic. It was just like always, off on a Sunday in the car for a little picnic. At the time, Duncan was seventy-five, and I was seventy. We went to St. Peters area and Larcheveque where some of his family still lived. It was a really nice fishing place that the old Morse Code operator, Mrs. MacKillop, had told me about. Beautiful spot. We go there now to pick cranberries in the fall.

18 Minutes

We would take an old tire and a pot to the beach for a picnic. We did that into the 1980s. The lobster was put in a pot with water and covered. The pot with the lobster would be placed in the middle of the old tire, and the tire was set on fire. It would be enough heat to cook the lobsters. We would go in swimming while the pot was boiling. In about eighteen minutes the lobsters would be cooking, steaming. We would crack the lobsters with the rocks. The lobsters didn't pick up the smell of the burning rubber. Lots of people did it. The tire would burn down, all the rubber would be gone, and only the wire would be left. We would throw those away. Good way to get rid of old tires. Now people have propane stoves, but that was one of the things we used to do when I wasn't working. It was a recreational thing. Even when the kids were away and came home to visit, we did it then. We definitely did it after the kids grew up.

We never had clambakes like they do in the Boston area. When I was twelve and thirteen we would make a little fire under a can down by the water and cook periwinkles. We would take the meat out of the shell with a common pin. Now I am not sure it would be clean enough. We were very careful, since it was a no-no to have fire.

Mi'kmaw Picnic Basket

I remember that in 1939, the Mi'kmaq Indians used to come into Sydney on a certain day of the week. People didn't know much about them then. They kept to themselves in their own communities. My husband Duncan's great-great-grandmother was a Mohawk Indian, but I don't think he knew that much about the tribe or their customs.

Over my lifetime, I have had very little contact with the Mi'kmaq people. There was no reservation anywhere near us. I didn't have occasion to meet many Mi'kmaw, but there is one thing that I do especially recall. Everyone in the village waited for them to come once a year to sell berry baskets and picnic baskets that they had made. They were very special, and everyone wanted one. The baskets were handmade, woven out of wood and decorated with sweet grass and bands of different colors. Some were painted. They probably cost 50 cents. They had picnic baskets, berry baskets, and sewing baskets with a cover on them.

My Husband Duncan Gray and Our Family

My husband Duncan's grandfather came from Larcheveque. The family lived in Sambro, N.S., and his grandfather came to Gabarus to run a lobster factory for H.E. Baker around the turn of the century. Duncan was the youngest of six living children.

Duncan and I worked together for our family. I was a major breadwinner with a good government job. Duncan made 15% as a lobster buyer, but it didn't add up to a lot of money. In our day, before 1990, the most we paid for lobster was 53 cents a pound.

Duncan would never say anything bad about anyone. My father was the same way. Gossip undermines community life. If you hear someone gossiping you know you can't trust them. Next they may be talking about you. In Gabarus, people have always seemed like they are on the same social level. There was no resentment when some people had more. People who had more always helped those who had less. I remember there was a poor family in Gabarus. They had lots of kids, and the father wasn't well. The little girl would sometimes knock on our door to see if we had some fat that we could share. We always did. Gladly.

Karen was born in 1942 and Nancy, born in 1945, was a baby when we moved back to Gabarus. When we came back we went to live in Duncan's childhood home with his mother and father. His father was only seventy-two when he died, one year after Duncan and I were married. We lived with Duncan's mother Elizabeth MacDonald Gray for fifteen years. I didn't have any disagreements with Mrs. Gray, but she was the head of the house. Duncan got along with her and helped me.

At the time she had a post office at the house, in the back where the kitchen is now. The post office at our house had no hours. People came whenever they wanted. At Christmas time, the packages were piled up higher than the windows with boxes and boxes of Eaton's purchases. People used the post office a lot more in those days. There was a lot of mail then, catalogue purchases, letters, and transactions. Now computer email has cut it all way way back.

LEFT TO RIGHT
DUNCAN GRAY, MILDRED GRAY, WAYNE DICKIE, FRED DICKIE, GRANT DICKIE. CA. 1961. MILDRED GRAY FAMILY PHOTOGRAPH. USED WITH PERMISSION.

Duncan was very good looking, kind, loving, with a good personality. Duncan was a good father and a good husband. He was never cross to the children. We had disagreements about money and other things but never any really big problems. Duncan was very good natured. Everybody liked him, including my mother Elsie.

Duncan had a great sense of humor. Duncan didn't fight or swear. Duncan was always generous. Years ago, Raymond Sutherland [next door] asked me and Duncan if Vivian's clothesline could go a bit into our property. He said "She can have her clothesline in our kitchen." No problem.

When Mrs. Gray became ill, she had two daughters who looked after her, and in 1958, she died at the age of 81. My life changed after that. We had to give up the post office, since I was on the telegraph then, and two government jobs were not allowed in one family.

Duncan was always generous and helpful. No one could have been better to my mother Elsie who lived with us for two years shortly before she died in The Cove in Sydney. Duncan said "Don't worry Middie, I'll take care of her." Elsie's health was good, but she had dementia. Some days were good, but finally she needed the kind of full time care she could get at the nursing home.

Family and the Future 169

Duncan's Best Fudge Recipe Ever

Duncan was not only a wonderful loveable man, he made the best chocolate fudge ever.

Duncan's Fudge Recipe

4 cups white sugar
1 cup of canned evaporated milk
2 heaping tablespoons of cocoa

Stir constantly over medium heat until it makes a soft ball when a spoonful is dropped in water.

Add a tablespoon of butter and a teaspoon of vanilla.

Take off stove and beat vigorously with a wooden spoon until it starts to harden. Pour into an 8 by 8 pan and let it set until ready to be cut into blocks.

Duncan never left the stove when he was cooking fudge. He kept an eye on it the whole time.

It was really good and shiny on the top. You could almost see your face in it.

The Day Duncan Died

Duncan died on a fine summer day, June 5, 1990. At 7:30 a.m. he left the house and went down to the wharf. He drove our new car, new to us, not even a year old. I was at home alone baking bread. About 8:30, less than an hour after he left home, my cousin Herb Reid who was a retired Methodist minister came to tell me that there was an accident. I asked, "What happened? He said "It's Duncan. He is dead."

Duncan drowned right off the wharf in Gabarus when his car went over into the water. Duncan was retired at the time, but had gone down to help the man who was taking over our lobster buying business. The transmission stuck, and the car went out 50 feet into the water. It all happened fast. Duncan tried to get out of the back window. Duncan drowned. Perhaps he was dead before he drowned. He may have had a heart attack. There was water in his lungs. The car was halfway across the barachois. He was wearing a nylon down-lined jacket. It got very heavy when it was wet, but I think it kept him afloat after.

They had already taken him in an ambulance and taken the car out of the water with rope. I never heard anything, not a thing, not even the ambulance. My doctor was a close friend, Dr. Ormiston. His grandfather is the man my father was named after. As soon as he found out that Duncan died, he said: "I'll be out within the hour, and I'll bring you something." I said, "I'll see it through. Don't bring me anything. I have strength enough and my senses to carry on." For me, I don't believe in tranquilizers and that kind of stuff. You have to have strength to overcome grief and bad things that come upon everyone in their life. Going through it, you get strength from God. You don't get it out of pills.

Five minutes after Herb came, my home was full of people coming to support me. My children were all away, living their own lives. My oldest Karen had just found out that she had leukemia. Albert was in Germany, Karen was in Calgary, and Nancy was in Dartmouth. All my relatives and friends came. It helped so much to bear the tragedy to have people around and supporting.

Duncan had a small insurance policy, but it is a lot of expense to die, a funeral and casket. People gave money to help out. My best friend Margaret MacDonald and a lot of people helped out with the funeral at Gabarus United Church. Everyone couldn't get into the church. His was the biggest funeral at the old church, with 1,040 signing the book. We knew everyone from here to St. Peters.

When Duncan died, it was so terrible it was unbelievable. Duncan was seventy-five when he died, but at the time he looked about fifty and had no grey hair. It has been 23 years since Duncan died in his shocking accident. I'll never get over the shock, although I made up my mind to get over the grief. The grief diminished some, but the shock never did. Maybe that's why my hands shake. But you do what you have to do. I wouldn't go out on that wharf for the world. I have an awful fear. Thank God time heals.

I went to Germany for the end of the year to Baden Baden where Albert was at the Canadian Airforce Base. I traveled around the area with Albert and his wife Marilyn, and I spent Christmas there that year. That was one of five times I traveled to Germany.

My Children

Duncan and I were very fortunate. We had three wonderful children. Karen was born in 1942. Nancy was born 1945, and Albert was born in 1947.

I think children should live their own life, especially with good grounding from childhood. And they have. They are all hardworking people and great parents. Albert joined the Air Force at 16. He graduated early, since his birthday was in November. He was good in math and studied and taught electronics. He is retired now, and he and his wife Marilyn live in the Annapolis Valley.

When Nancy was seventeen, she went out west with Herb Reid, a cousin of ours who was a minister in Calgary. Nancy lived there for ten years. She had graduated from Cape Breton Business College and worked as a secretary. That is where she met her husband Wayne Dickie. My daughter Karen went out West too and still lives there with her husband Tom Ferguson. Nancy's son Freddy was born in Calgary, and then Nancy and Wayne moved to southern Alberta. Wayne was in the Army, and he went overseas for six months to Greece. Then he was back for six months. My son Albert was also stationed in British Columbia.

Just like always, children follow in the same track as their parents. We were imprinted with responsibility and competence. I have seven wonderful accomplished grandchildren and eleven great-grandchildren and two great-great-grandchildren. I am still very close to my sister Freda's three daughters: Sandra, Gail and Faye in Arizona and their children too.

I am blessed with a truly wonderful family.

LEFT TO RIGHT
KENNETH SHERWOOD, MILDRED GRAY, TIM WHITE, LILLIAN HARRISS, TERRIN WHITE, LISA GALANOV AND JACQUELINE HOLMES, 2010. MILDRED GRAY FAMILY PHOTOGRAPH.
USED WITH PERMISSION.

Staying Physically and Emotionally Flexible

I am a big believer in the value of exercise. I used to ride my stationary bike every day for fifteen or twenty minutes a day. When you get old, you also have to be careful with walkers, if you need one. Walkers cause people to bend over. You should adjust it, so you aren't bent over. Same thing with grocery store carts. You should always get in the habit of straightening up. If you are in the habit of straightening up, then when you are old you won't be hunched over.

Gabarus has always been a great place for rowing. Grandpa Grant would take us in his little boat. That is why I like to kayak, since I was a rower for so many years. Rowers can easily be kayakers. I rowed a boat for a long time.

When I was out in a kayak with Tim White [from Rising Tide Expeditions] we went out into the [Gabarus] Bay when the *Bluenose* was on a tour. I was able go alongside and to touch the Bluenose name on the stern. That made me very happy.

174   Bringing Out the Untold Life

My father's father, Captain John Grant, was great for exercise. He was always exercising and always after us to exercise. When I was five years old, my Grandpa Grant taught me and a friend how to swim. On the trapeze in his fish house, we used to turn over and turn back. We called the game "skin the cat." In his fish house, he also had a see-saw kind of board between four ropes, like a bench swinging. We used to also play "go through the broom" holding a broomstick in both hands at each end and starting with it behind you, put it over your head and put each foot up over. I think it was something he saw or knew about. You had to be very flexible to do it.

Fortunately at my age I am still physically, and I hope emotionally, flexible. I can still bend over and touch the floor. Since growing up with my grandfather, I was introduced to fitness as a child and always maintained that. I take good care of myself, but I also know that when God calls me, I'll be happy to go. It is up to Him.

Nine Decades of Changes to Land and Sea

I have lived through significant changes in the environment. When I was little we used to play here and there in sandy coves, but now the sea has taken away a lot of the land and left rock. Places where we used to play and swim behind the island [Rouse Island] are not the same at all. There was once a little private beach where we could take the babies in their carriages. It was called Angel's Retreat, a unique place since colonial times that really should have been protected along with the [Louisbourg] fortress. There was a military hospital over there that was used by both the French and the English in both takings of Louisbourg. This is all gone, along with at least two to three meters of the land. The tides are much higher than they were even ten or fifteen years ago. And there is so much more erosion because of the higher tides, storms in Gabarus, and all along the coast of Cape Breton.

The ice cap is melting, and it will never be the same. It has made a big difference here in the village. Fifty or sixty years ago there was a lot more snow, and the lakes froze solid. Now we have hardly any winter and hardly any snow. Now you have to go into the woods to get enough snow to cross country ski or to snowshoe. The lakes don't freeze like they used to. The lakes are saltier and don't freeze as much or as long.

In those days we had a lot of snow. The snow was so high; it was sometimes up to the second story of our homes. There used to be high snow banks covering the fences that almost everyone had to hold their cows in. There were snow banks as early as Halloween then. Now, no snow banks. In those days, there was no snow plow. The men of the village would shovel the main road.

Snow was so much fun. There were so many things to do in the snow. Kids used to jump off the roof of our greenhouse into the snow bank, and we made snow houses. We had a lot of fun with ice skating, ice boats and hockey games. We had so many great skaters in the village.

When I was five years old, my grandfather Captain John Grant gave me a pair of wood skis. They were the right size for my age, about three or four feet long, and they curved way up at the front end. We had a picket fence. When it snowed I could ski over it.

We always had drift ice in April from the Bay of St. Lawrence. For the past four or five years we haven't had ice clampers, big pieces of ice in the bay. We have no drift ice now. When I was a little girl, we used to jump from one ice pan to another in the barachois. Grammy Reid, my mother's mother, lived at the end of the road right by the beach. She would be at the fence yelling at us: "Don't jump there!" You couldn't get an ice pan in there now.

What's Next

I have seen a lot of changes over the years, even language, so many new words now, connected with computers and technology. Everything is different now. The technology has gone beyond anything we could have imagined or only imagined in the funny papers.

It is almost impossible to understand how so many changes can occur in ninety years. Time goes by so fast. What's left to invent? Some technology? You can work in one country and live in another. We have advanced in computers; we have gone to the moon and back. That's good enough. Never mind trying to live on the other planets. Cloning of sheep worked, now they are trying to clone humans, but I don't think it is right. Scientists are playing God. That's going too far. There needs to be something mysterious.

MILDRED GRAY ON PORCH
AT HOME. CA. 2008.
MILDRED GRAY FAMILY
PHOTOGRAPH.
USED WITH PERMISSION.

Secrets to Longevity

I have a lot of longevity in my family. My great-grandfather William Grant lived to be ninety, and my great-grandmother Mary lived to be one hundred and one. My father Wiley died in 1965 at the age of eighty-one, and my mother lived to ninety-eight. I was forty-five when my father died, and I was sixty-eight when my mother died. Luckily I had my parents with me for a lot of my adult life. I was with both of them when they died.

My secrets to longevity? Exercise is one of them! Last year when I was in the hospital, I exercised every night. That is how I have kept strong and limber.

My advice is don't be ashamed to cry. It is good for you. When you are sad and you cry, you feel things deeply. And that is a good thing. I get emotional if a bird dies. When my cat died I nearly gave up. It was emotionally tough on me to handle the telegrams, happy and sad telegrams. I knew when people were suffering, more so than others.

There is a time for weeping and a time for joy. It comes naturally when you are depressed and thinking about how to solve a problem. I think it is good to feel feelings. I am easily hurt. Crying lets the air in to refresh your emotions. I truly feel other people's pain and suffering. I feel compassion. And I tried to help people.

How do I explain being strong in all kinds of situations?
> *Hard work and dedication to my work;*
> *Wholesome food—not too much;*
> *Strong character;*
> *Resilience. I can handle loss well;*
> *Probably don't let myself get upset over little things;*
> *Not afraid to be sensitive, emotional; and*
> *Humility, faith and perspective.*

You never know how people will turn out and what influences will impact them. People in Gabarus looked out for each other, and they still do. I was in contact with everyone, including people who were suffering. I tried to help people as much as I could. One family's house burned down. They needed help and everyone rallied to assist. I'll never forget.

My legacy? I hope I did some good. When I think of my life, at my age, working hard, trying to do the best I could with very little money.

I tried to help as many people as I could. I like to learn something every day. I have always been open to learning something new. Still am.

Summing Up

I can see beauty in the quiet life, the simple life. That is what we knew. We had good education, lots of recreation and very supportive family and friends around us. We had plenty of love, food, good health, clothes and faith. What else is there? There are people who are financially rich, but they may not have what we had. Everyone here helps each other. That is way it has always been.

In Gabarus, everyone seemed happy although they didn't have much. People got married and had a supper. People were contented and happy and loving and sharing with each other. They depended on each other. Now, people want new stuff. People aren't happy unless they have things. That is one big change in nine decades.

If you lose interest in life or what is happening in the world that is not good. The world is so small. At one time no one went anywhere. They only knew where they lived. Now we see how other people are living, especially in other countries, clothes, what they eat. It gives you a bigger perspective and something to think about. You can talk about it. Your world is not defined by the bounds of your own house.

I really care about people. I care about what happens to them. I wanted to share their joys and sorrows. I like to think that I was a help to people.

Life changed for me and for everyone after the end of the switchboard but I have stayed connected to the community. My home is still a center of the community. I love people, and I think they know that.

People trusted me and they still do. I am so lucky that I can remember. I hope that I am still a bridge with the past history of this place and the families, even people who moved away. So many people come back to visit, wanting to connect with their roots.

The linemen I worked with are grandfathers now, and I still see them. I hear about them and their families. A seventy-five year old man came to visit whose father was a minister here. He wanted to talk about when he was a little boy of five years old when he lived in Gabarus.

Everyone has a problem somewhere in their lives. You have to stay strong. The sun will come out, and you can close a chapter. Like everyone I had a lot of bad memories too. I try not to think about how old I am. I am still so interested in the world.

GRANT GRAY FAMILY REUNION. 2005. MILDRED GRAY FAMILY PHOTOGRAPH. USED WITH PERMISSION.

What is the Future of Gabarus?

We all hope that Gabarus will be renewed in population like it was in the early 1900s. We are getting a lot of new residents now who are contributing to the culture, civic life, and the character of the place. Also, the technology available now is playing a great role, making a contribution in improving communication with the rest of the world. Everyone has computers now. It is certainly a different world than the one in which I was brought up: Facebook, Internet, so much new technology has developed since the beginning of wireless in 1902.

People who come from here can now be in good touch with what is going on, and they can support initiatives to improve the community. We can communicate easily with people all over the world, and the voice of fewer than one hundred people in Gabarus can influence people all over.

Now you can also learn how people all over the world are living. It brings us closer together as humans. In my day you had to travel to see for yourself. I lived through all those decades of development in communication.

Family and the Future   183

It can change people's lives, no matter what country people are living in. It helps people in other countries. As people of the world we can educate, and be educated, about some of the extreme, painful conditions and traditions. Communication shines a light on issues across the globe and helps people to see how other people are living. It shows their common humanity.

When I was a little girl I didn't know much about what was happening in other parts of the world. Now a child in kindergarten in Cape Breton might be talking on Skype with children in Indonesia. The whole idea of pen pals has a different potential now. Education is the key to the use of this modern technology. People all over the world have a chance to compare and to evaluate their own customs and beliefs. Literacy and women's rights will be more universal through the exchange of ideas. People the world over can have a better existence and way of life. We will all be one after a while, all one human race.

People have it within them to discern what is authentic and what is true. A lot of jealousy, competition and hatred, especially in politics, gets in the way of good will among people. I also believe that stress and competition contribute to mental illness. It's not good for you. There is too much of that now. Technology in the end will bring people together more. They will trade their ideas, some good and some bad. Eventually we'll all be wiser.

I believe that God is everywhere. I have no fear. Trust in God makes all things possible. God sends people to help. I have great faith in prayer. It may not be answered the way you think it should be, but it is answered in the most beneficial way to the person who asked for guidance. Everything happens for a purpose. That is what I believe. If there is a last word, it is that I trust in God and in prayer. Try it!

HIGHLIGHTS OF GABARUS HISTORY

Highlights of Gabarus History

The recollections of Mildred Reid Grant Gray and the history of Gabarus cannot be separated from the past seven centuries of the history of Cape Breton Island, Fortress Louisbourg, the international fishing trade, and the 20th century communications revolution. What follows are brief highlights of some of the salient context issues that Mrs. Gray's recollections have referenced. This section is necessarily limited in scope to the Gabarus area. There is a great deal more to learn about Cape Breton Island and its many-faceted history. *Highlights of Gabarus History* is not intended to be wholly comprehensive, but rather a substantive starting point for further study.

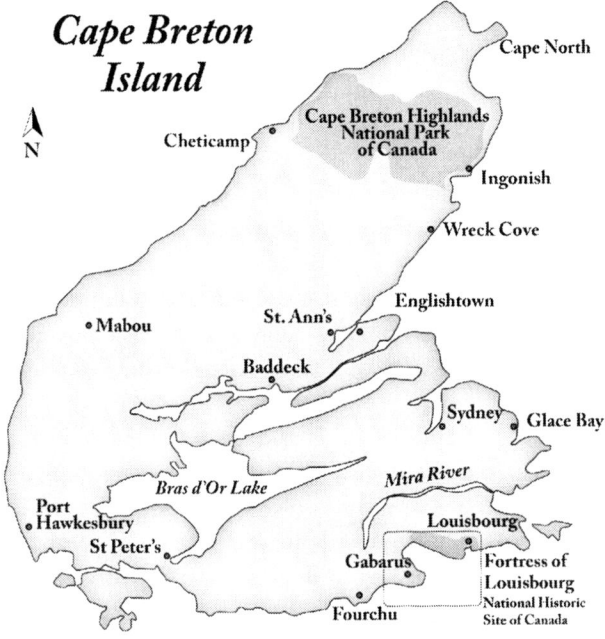

Cape Breton Island in Eastern Canada is less than one mile northeast of mainland Nova Scotia, "close enough to the mainland to be influenced by what goes on there, but far enough away to have developed its own ways."[4]

For the first 35 years of Mildred Gray's life, the Island was only accessible by boat or plane. In that period of Mrs. Gray's early life, there was a train ferry that connected Cape Breton towns including Louisbourg, Glace Bay, and Sydney to the mainland and beyond.

In 1955, Cape Breton Island was connected to mainland Nova Scotia by the Canso Causeway, but Cape Breton still remains a true island and one of the most beautiful in the world according to *Condé Nast Traveler* and *Travel+Leisure Magazine.* It was designated one of *National Geographic Traveler*'s Best Trips of 2013.

Cape Breton is a place noted for its historic interest and warm hospitality and is renowned for its beautiful natural scenery. Author Dorothy Duncan sang its praises over 70 years ago, and her description still rings true.

> *Cape Breton is a distilled essence of loveliness...more like a lullaby, modest and withdrawn. It is a refuge-as, in a sense, all islands are...And because it has always respected its guests, Cape Breton remains a refuge for anyone in need of the solace of tranquility.*[5]

The fine character of Cape Bretoners is legend. Lady Aberdeen, the wife of the Governor General of Canada, made an official visit to Cape Breton in 1897 and said that "nowhere have we met simpler, gentler, more hearty folk than these."[6] To its residents, Cape Breton Island also affords a powerful sense of identity and place, as we can readily tell from reading Mrs. Gray's recollections.

Cape Breton Island has a distinctive history. Based on archeological evidence[7], historians believe that the first residents of Cape Breton were ancestors of the Mi'kmaq, the only inhabitants of the island at the time of European discovery. According to the Mi'kmaq Resource Centre at Cape Breton University,

> *The Micmacs*[8] *were not startled by the appearance of early explorers in sailing ships. They had been expecting them, since according to legend 'blue-eyed people would arrive from the east to disrupt their lives'.*[9]

By the time the first colonists arrived, the Mi'kmaq had had many years of interaction with European fishermen.

188   Bringing Out the Untold Life

It is likely that Biarne Heriulfason went off course along the coast of Cape Breton in 986 when trying to join his father at the Norse settlement in Greenland. Based on his description, "it may have been some part of the southern coast of Cape Breton."[10] Fourteen years later [in 1000 AD] Leif Ericsson, a son of Eric the Red, "made a voyage to find the lands of which Biarne had brought home vague reports." [11] These explorers are almost universally believed to have been the first Europeans the Mi'kmaq saw, although "they left no traces."[12] Ample archeological evidence does point to Norse settlements in Greenland and L'Anse-aux-Meadows on the north coast of Newfoundland.

The next Europeans were the intrepid Basque fishermen who made seasonal, and secret, visits as early as 1372.[13]

> *The Basques were unique, a people whose homeland straddled the French-Spanish border yet who were neither French nor Spanish, with a language and ethnic heritage absolutely distinct from both.* [14]

According to historian Christopher Moore, the Basques have two "touchstone values: *indarra* (strength, power and physical good health) and *sendoa* (its spiritual equivalent expressed in strength of character, stoicism, and dedication)."[15] These values supported them in their fearless travels across the Atlantic Ocean, and there is ample proof of the primacy of the Basque sailors in opening up cod fishing in the New World including the place name evidence of Cape Breton and Gabarus.

The seas of the North Atlantic have the justified reputation of being among the most richly-stocked fishing grounds in the world. Early Basque, Breton, Portuguese and Norman sailors were looking for cod and whale, both plentiful in the North Atlantic. In fact, Cape Breton had greater density of cod than anything ever seen in Europe; "this was the Basques' secret."[16]

These sailors of Western Europe who traveled to the rich fishing grounds and returned to their homes in the winter were in no hurry to let others know where they were going and how they were getting there. Over the 16th and 17th century they also made documented trips. "The elders of the community could boast forty or fifty voyages to Terre-Neuve, six to eight months of the year devoted to the catching and shipping of precious cod."[17]

In 1497, five years after Columbus's expeditions to the Caribbean, Henry VII commissioned Giovanni Caboto [now called John Cabot], a Venetian merchant living in Bristol, England, to explore the new world for Britain. Caboto and Columbus were nationality and age peers, having been born in Genoa, Italy, in about the same year. According to author Mark Kurlansky, they probably knew each other.[18]

Caboto was traveling from Bristol for thirty-five days west across the Atlantic when he saw "a long rocky coastline teeming with cod."[19] Historian C. Bruce Fergusson, formerly Nova Scotia's provincial archivist, cited some "evidence that Cape Breton Island was the place that John Cabot and his son Sebastian first saw and named 'New Founde Land', most likely the easternmost cape of Cape Breton [Gabarus]."[20] Among other historians, this is not a widely held opinion, since there is no hard evidence to prove exactly what land Cabot found or where he landed.

An Italian who was visiting in England heard about Cabot's voyage and said that "the sea is covered with fishes, which are caught not only with a net but with baskets, a stone being tied to them in order that the baskets may sink in the water."[21] There are so many descriptions of the extraordinary abundance of codfish. *The Story of Framboise* [near Gabarus] describes the early Scots' settlement in the mid-19th century and notes that: "codfish were so plenty then that if you'd stick a net out from the rocks, it would be loaded."[22] This is consistent with a striking statement from a 1873 book by Alexandre Dumas quoted by Mark Kurlansky.

> *It has been calculated that if no accident prevented the hatching of the eggs and each egg reached maturity, it would take only three years to fill the sea so that you could walk across the Atlantic dryshod on the backs of cod.*[23]

Fishing for the plentiful cod drove the development of the area. As a result of Cabot's voyage in 1497, Britain claimed the North American coast, although British settlement in North America hadn't begun in Jamestown, until 1607.

Especially at the very beginning of the 16th century, fishing really opened up in the area "with the enthusiasm of a gold rush of 1501", and "by the mid 1500s 60 percent of all the fish eaten in Europe was cod."[24] Fishing remained the foundation of the

Cape Breton economy, and from the 16th and well into the 20th centuries cod was the most important species of fish. The cod fishery became France and England's great economic interest in North America, "more valuable than the fur trade, source of an important foodstuff, great employer of ships and men."[25]

The potential for the cod catch in the New World drew men from the Atlantic coast of Europe to sail westward by the thousands. Historians note that most of the fishermen were seasonal migrant workers who came for a six-month season of fishing often "enduring half a year of privation to earn half a year in the security of his ancestral home."[26]

> *From Basque seaports in southwestern France, from Brittany and the Channel ports of Normandy, flotillas of tiny fishing boats and larger merchantmen were sailing west, crammed with supplies for a season's work, crammed also with fishermen and shore laborers.*[27]

By the end of the 16th and 17th centuries, the British and French fishermen in the seas around Cape Breton had begun to come ashore to dry their catch.[28] As a result, there was more contact with the Mi'kmaq, and each season the Mi'kmaq "would bring furs to the fishing stations [like Gabarus] located on Cape Breton's east coast."[29] The Europeans and their market for furs had changed the hunting habits of the Mi'kmaq. In the 17th century, Nicholas Denys remarked that before the demands of the European fur trade, the Mi'kmaq "did not lack animals, which they killed only in proportion as they had need for them."[30] After the arrival of the Europeans, the Mi'kmaq actively traded fur for metal cooking utensils and other supplies.

In particular, beginning in the early 17th century the French had a close friendship with the Mi'kmaq. Grand Chief Membertou and his extended family had been converted to Catholicism in 1610 by a French Jesuit priest. That same year, they forged a treaty with the Vatican, *The Concordat of 1610*. As political and spiritual allies of the Mi'kmaq, the French were able to benefit from peaceful relations, support, and the Mi'kmaw communication system, runners "who went from village to village relaying messages about recent or future events, treaties entered into, and even calls to war."[31]

We can be certain that the early fishermen from all of these countries [Spain, Portugal, England, and France] would have been fishing in the vicinity of Gabarus and Fourchu. The fishermen who had been coming for centuries certainly would have noticed the island's rich resources of wood, fresh water, and sheltered harbors, especially around places like Gabarus and Louisbourg. So it is no surprise that it was one of the first areas settled when the French colony was established. At the same time, historians posit that "it must have been a fairly congenial international community in spite of the continuing wars between England, France, and Spain."[32]

The value of dried codfish grew very quickly as a staple commodity in Europe. At the same time, the French and English realized that they would need permanent settlements from which fish could be readily caught and dried for shipment to Spain, Portugal, and the West Indies. "Ignoring the natives, royal governments were ready to grant exclusive rights to the fishery and fur trade to those willing to pay for them, and willing to transport settlers to North America."[33]

During the colonial era, the fisheries employed "tens of thousands of fishermen from numerous European countries."[34] Thus the fishing trade sustained the fishermen who visited or settled in Louisbourg, Gabarus, Fourchu and the surrounding area for more than 500 years.

Cod, the Wonder Fish

By all accounts, the Atlantic cod (gadus morhua) is an extraordinary fish, beautiful, hardy and prolific. Mrs. Gray also remembers when cod was the most important fish being harvested in the waters off Gabarus. She and her neighbors in Gabarus and other nearby fishing communities, may be some of the few people who know what real fresh Atlantic cod tastes like.

The historical and scientific literature on cod and its impact on human history is almost as bountiful as the cod itself once was. The story of cod is a fascinating tale of the impact of one commodity on world history, world economies, and human endeavor. One of the most comprehensive and readable works on the subject is Mark Kurlansky's 1997 book *Cod: The Tale of The Fish that Changed the World*.

He provides us with some meaningful information about the plentiful fish that so affected the development of Gabarus and Cape Breton. Kurlansky notes that: "Cod is a wonder fish." When dry, cod is 80 percent protein, and it has virtually no fat.[35] It is a hardy fish, "made to endure" since it is especially "resistant to parasites and diseases".[36] Further, the cod fish adapts its diet depending on what is available, and it "will eat almost anything".[37] One particularly extraordinary fact is the prolific nature of the cod. Kurlansky reports that "a 40-inch female cod can produce three million eggs in a spawning.[38] This sounds like a recipe for overabundance, but very few eggs survive. "If each female cod produces two juveniles that live to be sexually mature adults, the population is stable."[39] The cod became vulnerable because of another aspect of its nature, to live on the ocean floor, its safe place. That is why cod was "rendered commercially extinct by bottom draggers."[40]

As we have described, cod was the reason for the European expansion, and its rich supply was sustained for centuries. Noted Canadian biologists Jeffrey Hutchings and Ransom Myers observed that "the vastness of the [cod] resource led many to believe that it was inexhaustible."[41]

Very unfortunately, the cod resource was not inexhaustible nor the fish hardy enough to withstand the intense overfishing that led to the collapse of the cod fisheries in the 1990s. Approximately 8 million tons of cod were harvested in the 250 years between 1500 and 1750, the same amount harvested in the 15 years between 1960 and 1975.[42]

In 1992 the Canadian government declared a moratorium on the cod fishery that, for well over 500 years, had largely shaped the lives and communities of Canada's eastern coast. The commercial extinction of cod "was, and remains, an ecological disaster of extraordinary magnitude."[43] Cod's capacity to renew itself is still threatened, but there are starting to be some modest signs of a cod comeback. In 2011, Canadian Geographic reported on research findings in the journal Nature that theorized that the moratorium on cod fishing was starting to show results, although the cod that are coming back are smaller, only about 60 percent of the weight it was in the 1980s.[44]

Chaloupe, Shallop

The humble chaloupe, a boat of Basque origins, played a pivotal role in development of Cape Breton and Gabarus.

Small boat fishing via the chaloupe, or shallop as it is called in English, was the heart of the cod fishing industry. The Basque used it as a whaleboat as well as for cod fishing. In much of the historical literature, the term shallop is used interchangeably with "whaleboat", most likely since the nautical design was descended from European shallops.[45] In Herman Melville's *Moby Dick*, he describes Captain Ahab "standing in his shallop's stern."[46]

The shallop was by far the main boat used by the fishermen of Gabarus and Cape Breton throughout the 16-19th centuries and likely earlier. Shallops are open wooden workboats of about 30 feet (9 meters) long that are powered by both oars and sails.[47] The foremast is placed far forward, and the main mast far behind to leave space in the middle for storing the fish. The rigging for the sails is portable, so that the masts can be readily taken down, and the boat is light enough to be dragged up onto the beach. It can travel in deep or shallow water.

Fishermen report that this boat is highly maneuverable, since its shallow keel allows it to come very close to shore. The shallop also has a lot of capacity to transport the fish after they are caught. According to historian Stephen Hornsby, each day, "if the cod were biting, as many as 3-4 quintals (hundredweight) would be taken in [a shallop] by each fisherman."[48] Traditionally, the small shallops operating out of Gabarus, and the other settlements along the coast, would have had three, undoubtedly strong, men on each boat and probably another two on shore to cure the cod catch.[49] The shallops came ashore each day, and the catch would be cleaned and salted for several days, then washed well, and laid out to dry on flakes[50], just as Mrs. Gray describes it.

> *By 1740, there were 48 schooners, 393 chaloupes, and 2,445 fishermen employed in the fisheries of Île Royale [Cape Breton]. Each chaloupe carried 3-4 men, and the catch per boat averaged 300 quintals (quintal=hundredweight) per summer season.*[51]

Like today, fishermen worked every day they could, and "every trip tested the seamanship, skill and endurance of the three man crew."[52] Once the fishermen found a good place to fish, they would take down the sails, anchor the boat or drift over the fish bank, dropping as many of their multi-hooked lines as they could manage. Hired fishermen were paid for what they caught, so they would work diligently all day, pulling in the lines and tossing the fish into compartments in the middle floor of the shallop. This kind of fishing was going for well over two hundred years before the establishment of the fortress at Louisbourg.

Still in use late into the 1800s, "Cape Breton-crafted shallops used for in-shore fishing were …far more numerous than the larger off-shore vessels, numbering more than 3,000 in 1884 and manned by over 6,700 men."[53]

Capbreton to Cape Breton

The earliest known map of North America was drawn by a Basque mapmaker, Juan de la Costa[54] and the name "Cape Breton" is the "oldest European place name transferred to America, appearing on the Portuguese map of 1516-20."[55]

Cape Breton Island is almost certainly named after the commune of Capbreton on the far southwest coast of France, since its shores are on almost the same latitude "which was the primary method of navigation."[56] In fact, the latitude of Capbreton is 43.6430° N, and the latitude of Gabarus, Cape Breton is 45.8372° N.

How Gabarus Got Its Name: A Bay, a Lake, and a Fishing Port

Multiple sources point to the fact that Gabarus is named after the Cabarrus family who made their home in Capbreton, France.[57] An additional and compelling source is the Cabarrus family history, some excerpts of which follow, with a translation in English.[58]

> C'est lui [Barthélémy Cabarrus: 1681-1733] qui…vers 1720 environ, va marquez de son nom le territoire Canadien. Il baptisera Cabarrus un morceau de la côte du territoire de l'île du Cap-Breton, en Nouvelle Ecosse, au large d l'embouchure du Saint-Laurent. Il y a maintenant là bas un lac, une baie et un petit port de pêche qui portent tous le nom de Cabarrus, devenu Gabarus.[59]

> It is he [Barthélémy Cabarrus: 1681-1733] who… around 1720, will leave his name as a mark on a Canadian territory. He will baptize as "Cabarrus" a piece of the Cape Breton coast in Nova Scotia, off the mouth of the St. Lawrence. At present, the location boasts a lake, a bay, and a small fishing port, all of which bear the name Cabarrus, transformed into Gabarus.

L'acte d'anoblissement que Louis XVI donnera
à la famille en 1789 stipule bien que Barthélémy
a laissé son nom à ce coin de terre. Mais l'a-t'il
fait seulement en vertu de ses propres mérites ou
plutôt en souvenir d'un de ses ancètres qui avait
donné a sa découverte le nom de sa ville natale.
Les Capbretonnais répètent une légend tenace
qui veut que ce soient des Capbretonnais, dont un
Cabarrus qui aient découvert les terres lointaines de
l'Amerique, des "terres neuves" lors d'une chassse à
la baleine. Ils auraient baptise l'ile ainsi découverte
du nom de luer port d'attache: Ile de Capbrreton…
bien sur avant que Christophe Columb ne touchât le
sol l'Amérique.[60]

The grant of nobility given to the [Cabarrus] family by Louis XVI in 1789 confirms that Barthélémy left his name to this corner of the earth. However, it remains an open question whether he [King Louis XVI] did this [granted nobility] only by reason of his [Barthélémy's] own merits, or rather in recognition of his [Barthélémy's] ancestors who had given to his discovery [the whole island] the name of his home town. Those from capbreton [the village in France, about 10 miles -16 km north of Bayonne] repeat a stubborn legend that it was their people ["capbrettonais" meaning people from the French village], of whom one was a Cabarrus, who discovered faraway lands in America, new lands discovered during a hunt for whales. They named the island thus discovered after their original home port. The Island of Cape Breton [was discovered] well before Christopher Columbus touched American soil.

And this account seems quite plausible.[61] Barthélémy Cabarrus and his family were very successful merchants and ship owners. He once said that he was only at home for two months of the year, and the rest of the time he was "at sea on fishing vessels …. or in service to the [French] King."[62] Barthélémy Cabarrus began trading with Louisbourg beginning when the fortress was first built beginning in 1714, and he did so until his death in 1733.

According to research conducted by Gabarus community historians Tim Menk and Gene Kersey, the trade was continued by his son and two grandsons until 1758, when the French lost the Fortress and Cape Breton to the English. "The grandsons were seized, along with the French-owned ship they were aboard when it tried to run the English naval blockade."[63]

Barthélémy's granddaughter Thérésia was the celebrated and very colorful Madame Cabarrus Tallien, called Notre-Dame de Thermidor in honor of her role as a symbol of the end of terror during the French Revolution. Her son, Barthélémy's great-grandson, Edouard (Tallien de) Cabarrus, was a friend of Honoré Balzac, Victor Hugo, and Alexandre Dumas. He was Napoleon III's doctor and was also considered one of the best homeopaths of his day.

Surely, there is much more to explore about the naming of Cape Breton Island, Gabarus, and the extraordinary Cabarrus family. Overall, a notable family name that still lives well in Cape Breton on a bay, a lake, and a fishing port.

Sister Settlements: Gabarus and Louisbourg

Gabarus and Louisbourg have an intimate historic connection. Located on the east coast of Cape Breton Island, Gabarus and Louisbourg are on opposite sides of Gabarus Bay, an area that has had a central role in the exploration and colonization of North America over the centuries. Gabarus is on the south side of the Bay, and Louisbourg on the north. By the old road originally established by the French between the two settlements in 1751[64] it is 12 miles (east to west).[65] This is the road on which Mrs. Gray traveled to Louisbourg on her bicycle when she was a child.

Gabarus Bay is "5 miles deep westward and nearly 5 miles wide at its entrance between White Point (northeast) and Cape Gabarus which bears southwestward from it."[66] The scenery, especially on the north side of the bay is strikingly picturesque. The area was, and is, both beautiful and rich in fish, wildlife, and berries. Two hundred years ago, the caribou roamed free and sea ducks abounded. "In 1805, Cape Breton government administrator A.C. Dodd reported sighting 1,500 caribou on the Gabarus barrens between Louisbourg and Gabarus."[67]

One hundred years later, in the early 1900s, C.W. Vernon noted that "streams and small lakes abound in which trout are plentiful," and "good shooting may be had all along the coast, especially in the spring, when sea ducks are to be found in large numbers."[68] As late as 1869, historian Richard Brown described "plenty of game and woodcocks [partridges] so extremely tame that you can knock them down with stones.[69]

A Temperate, Industrious and Thriving People

At various times during the period of European development in North America, Gabarus was one of the largest settlements in Cape Breton. Over the centuries it has often been described as "a beautiful village … splendidly located on a magnificent bay."[70] In 1903, when Gabarus had about 1,000 residents, Vernon noted that "the dwellings of the people are considerably above those of the average fishing settlement in capacity, comfort and appearance."[71]

Ten years later, Gabarus was similarly recognized for "its fine harbour and comfortable homes. The people are of fine old Loyalist stock, mostly fishermen, and own a fine fleet of boats [and] are evidently reaping a good harvest from the sea."[72] In 1920, the positive praise for the people and the place was further affirmed: "The fishermen, whose scattered houses are principally situated on the southern shores of the bay, are a temperate, industrious and thriving people."[73] Surely, this is still true today, in 2013.

Treaty of Utrecht in 1713

Although Gabarus, Louisbourg and Cape Breton Island have been visited for centuries by fishermen from western Europe, a lot changed for the area when England and France went to war over the succession to the Spanish throne. At the peace negotiations in the Dutch city of Utrecht, when the Treaty [of Utrecht] was signed in 1713, France lost mainland Nova Scotia but acquired the right to retain and fortify Cape Breton.[74] France moved rapidly to establish its settlements. The French left their home in Placentia, Newfoundland in the "late summer of 1713 with 149 settlers, including 116 men, 10 women and 23 children; and 100 soldiers sailing to Havre à l'Anglois [the future Louisbourg]."[75]

Subsequent to the establishment of Louisbourg after 1713, Gabarus, with its natural advantages for fishing proximity to cod and its capacity as a source of wood and agricultural products, became a settled fishing outport bound to Louisbourg by geographic nearness, common commerce, and significant political events.

Louisbourg became the site of a French fortress built to protect France's interests in the New World. It took twenty five years to build this "Dunkirk of America",[76] although, based on the outcome of two major assaults in the 18th century, the defenses of the Louisbourg Fortress seem to have been more imposing than effective. According to A.J.B. Johnston, "in reality, Louisbourg was not a fort. It was a town which began as a humble fishing port but which evolved into a European-style town."[77] Louisbourg's layout was actually similar to New Orleans, since both towns planned a church in a central place along the waterfront.[78]

Regardless of the various opinions about its design, the French invested huge sums of money in developing the site, and by 1738,

> *"Louisbourg was transformed from a cluster of huts at the edge of a spruce forest to a handsome town, a flourishing outpost of French civilization and the permanent home of some two thousand men, women and children."*[79]

Please keep in mind that in 1715, before the development of Louisbourg, the entire population of Cape Breton Island was only 720.[80]

Île-Royale [Cape Breton] rapidly became a leader in the increasing maritime trade. Within a few years of its founding, the new French colony was "producing and exporting stocks of cod worth about three times as much as Canada's annual beaver fur exports."[81] Between 1713 and 1745, the first period of French occupation, "over one half of all adults on Île Royale worked in the fishery, on either a seasonal or full time basis."[82]

Outports like Gabarus with protected harbours became fishery centers shortly after 1713.[83] According to numerous historians, at the time of the French colony, there was a large fishing station in Gabarus. Coastal shipping linked Louisbourg and Gabarus and the other outports, "most of which appear to have been economic satellites of the capital."[84] Under French rule both Gabarus and Fourchu were very busy in the fishing season. The fishing catch was brought ashore for salting and drying and ultimately shipped away, and "a great many small boats were built along the shore to carry out the work."[85]

In the early years of the 18th century before 1745, the heads of household came from four main areas: St. Malo, Placentia, Newfoundland, Southwest France (Basque country), and Midwest France, with the majority from St. Malo, a walled port city in Brittany in northwestern France on the English Channel.[86] St. Malo has an interesting history of independent spirit and was also the home of notorious French privateers and sometimes pirates. Explorer Jacques Cartier lived and sailed from Saint-Malo. Again, another area of interest and future study.

The fishery was most certainly the life blood of Île Royale. Fishermen lived on the island or returned annually to make their catch, as they had for over three hundred years. Some practiced "wet fishery" whereby the fish were caught and salted on the ship. The resident fishermen practiced "dry fishery" and salted and dried their fish on shore. Once dried, the fish didn't spoil and could be shipped long distances, as a high protein food for sailors traveling the world, and for slaves in the West Indies.

The area population grew rapidly. "By the 1740s the population of Louisbourg with its suburbs was close to 4,500 while that of the island as a whole was home to 10,000."[87]

Île Royale: Front Door of Canada

> In the 18th century, Gabarus Bay was the site of two sieges of Fortress Louisbourg, in 1745 and then again in 1758, turning points in the Anglo-French imperial struggle for what is today the nation of Canada.

Looking out on a peaceful Gabarus Bay today it is rather remarkable to imagine the scene of hundreds of ships and tens of thousands of seamen and soldiers who brought war to these shores. The people of Gabarus were witnesses to these events, although they likely fled into the woods. There is some mention of men in nearby communities, Baleine, Lorambec [Lorraine], and Niganiche [Ingonish] specifically, being called upon to form a small militia to support the French, and historians describe how the Mi'kmaq supported the French and fought on their behalf.[88]

First Siege of Louisbourg

The first siege of Louisbourg started on May 11, 1745, when more than 100 British colonial vessels including 4 large warships arrived in Gabarus Bay under the command of Lieutenant-General William Pepperrell, a prosperous Massachusetts merchant and politician.[89]

Pepperrell's orders were to destroy French "fishing vessels, houses, stages, flakes [racks for the drying of codfish], etc. throughout the island, to destroy the Cape Breton fishing industry whether or not Louisbourg was captured. "These orders were faithfully carried out…so that after three or four weeks no hamlet or settlement was left unravaged."[90] Several historians propose that some French settlers remained on the island by escaping into the woods, seeking shelter with other settlers or friendly Mi'kmaq.

The British colonials from New England were able to make a landing in spite of the fact that "the rocks and surf were more dangerous than the enemy."[91]

They then encircled the Fortress. The French called for the aid of the Mi'kmaq who were observed to be "very brave and warmly attached to the French."[92] According to Morgan, there was fighting in the outlying settlements. He did not say that Gabarus was one of them, but Gabarus is so proximate to Louisbourg that it is likely. On 28 June 1745, the 47-day siege ended when Fortress Louisbourg fell to the New Englanders.[93]

The New England colonists had to wait for British troops to relieve them, and winter and dysentery "killed 890 men, more than had died in the siege, and "one third of the garrison of around 2,000 was constantly sick."[94]

Aix-la-Chapelle in 1748 and the Birthplace of the American Nation

Less than two years after the British colonial conquest of Louisbourg in 1745, Great Britain agreed to give Louisbourg and Cape Breton (Île Royale) back to France in 1749 as part of the peace negotiations at Aix-La-Chapelle in 1748 related to the war of the Austrian succession.[95]

Returning Cape Breton Island to the French caused a great deal of bitterness among the New Englanders and the Englishmen.[96] **Historians note that Louisbourg could be said to be the birthplace of the American nation, where the seeds of discontent were sown that thirty years later blossomed into the American Revolution.**[97] The New Englanders didn't get the plunder they expected; they endured a terrible winter, and many died. "Those who survived went home to New England as potential agitators against British rule."[98] In fact, the same colonist, Lt. Col. Richard Gridley, "who planned the siege works at Louisbourg in 1745, laid out the trench system at Bunker Hill"…and there were other Louisbourg veterans at the Battle of Bunker Hill, fought on the 30th anniversary of the first siege of Louisbourg.[99]

Immediately after the Treaty of Aix-la-Chapelle, the French "rushed back to resettle and fortify Île Royale", taking possession on 23 July 1749.[100] According to Morgan, most area fishing settlements grew after 1749, likely Gabarus among them.

In the meantime, in 1755, the British deported the Acadians from Nova Scotia although apparently some managed to get back to Cape Breton and Isle Madame. In this colonial period, Gabarus continued to be a small settlement that grew substantially during the fishing season. From the census of 1752, nineteen residents were noted, mostly with French, Swiss, and Belgian backgrounds, residents named "Huiker, du Chambon, Baudry, Clermont, Daguerre, Tuillier, Durand, Duport, Metayer, and Rousseau."[101] We don't know with certainty, but many of these citizens were probably deported by the British after the second siege of Louisbourg. Again, the day-to-day experiences and the fate of these families is another area of attention for future historians of Gabarus.

Second Siege of Louisbourg

Formal hostilities broke out again in 1758 when a British combined army and naval force of 27,000 set sail in May 1758 to lay siege to Louisbourg.[102] Again, the ships sailed into Gabarus Bay. General James Wolfe led the British attack.[103]

As noted, the Mi'kmaq were allied with the French, and during the second siege of Louisbourg, they saw the British ships from Fourchu Harbour [south of Gabarus Bay] and ran to Louisbourg to warn the French: "The sight of Admiral Boscawen's fleet was no surprise to Drucour [Governor of the Fortress] and his officers. The Indians had come with the news that they had seen the fleet off Fourchu."[104] Surely the Mi'kmaq were extraordinary runners, getting there faster than the ships could sail!

The second siege of Louisbourg beginning on June 2, 1758 must have also been amazing for Gabarus residents to witness, although again they may have run as far as possible into the woods when they sighted the British navy and one hundred and fifty nine British vessels sailing into Gabarus Bay—"22 ships of the line, 17 frigates, 2 fire ships, and 118 transports" and Admiral Boscawen and Generals Amherst and Wolfe's land force of more than 12,000 men.[105]

The ships encountered thick fog and high waves, and French gunfire was so intense that General Wolfe was apparently ready to tell his men to retreat to the ships, but "he saw that many of the boats were already smashed on the rocks, and they went ahead with the invasion."[106]

The British defeated the French again, and "orders were given to destroy the other settlements on the island 'in a quiet way', but these orders seemingly were not obeyed."[107] The fortress itself was "systematically demolished in 1760 to prevent a French return."[108] However, "like the sea after a storm, the remaining inhabitants of the island settled down into as normal a way of life as was possible in their uncertain circumstances."[109]

Under the waters of Gabarus Bay and Louisbourg Harbour, the sieges of Louisbourg are still quietly remembered by numerous historic wrecks of naval vessels.

According to Robert Grenier: "In the harbour and surrounding areas there are at least twenty-six documented wrecks from the period 1713-1758."[110]

Mrs. Gray is directly descended from two soldiers who served in the British army during colonial times. Her 4th and 5th great-grandfather on her father's side, James Townsend [b. about 1740 at Greenwich, Kent, England, d. about 1804 at Louisbourg, NS] served in the British army for 23 years including at both the first and second sieges of Louisbourg, and he was in Quebec with General James Wolfe. James Townsend had two grants of land, a license for 400 acres of land on Louisbourg Harbour and a fishing lot, also on Louisbourg Harbour. James was discharged with the rank of Sergeant in 1759.[111]

William Bagnell [b. May 1731 at London, England, d. 1811 at Gabarus, NS] was Mrs. Gray's 4th great-grandfather. William Bagnell came to Cape Breton in 1758 as a Sergeant with the British Army under Gen. James Wolfe at the second siege of Louisbourg. After the war, he settled in Cape Breton and was the father of John Bagnell [b. 16 October 1767 at Louisbourg, NS, d. 1827] who was the father of William Henry Bagnell [b. 17 March 1798 at Gabarus, NS, d. 15 September 1860 at Gabarus, NS], listed as a native on the first census that included "Gabarouse."[112] Another of Mrs. Gray's 4th great-grandparents, Benjamin Cann [b. abt. 1739 at Bristol, England] from another seafaring family, is one of the earliest settlers of Gabarus.[113]

In 1928, the Fortress of Louisbourg was declared a National Historic Site of Canada. During the 1960s and 1970s, one fifth of the fortress was reconstructed and now serves as an outstanding living history museum.

Cape Breton, British Colony

The French governor of Louisbourg, Drucour, surrendered on 26 July 1758.[114] This marked the final end to French rule in Cape Breton. Again the French were rounded up and deported to France or to the islands of St. Pierre and Miquelon south of Newfoundland. Apparently, after the French left, some fishermen remained, and they were joined by English, Scottish and Irish settlers and Loyalists.

The British garrison of 300 stayed in Louisbourg until 1768, and merchants and fishermen from Newfoundland, many of Irish origin, settled there. Some members of the garrison settled near Louisbourg, like William Bagnell, one of the earliest settlers in Gabarus, Mrs. Gray's 4th great-grandfather.[115]

With the Treaty of Paris in 1763, Île Royale (Cape Breton Island) and her sister Île St. Jean (Prince Edward Island) came under the rule of the British.[116] The Seven Years' War [French and Indian War] had come to an end, and France "lost all her possessions in North America except the colony of Louisiana and the islands of St. Pierre and Miquelon."[117]

Samuel Holland, Dutch born British officer, who conducted a survey between 1764 and 1767 claimed that there were only "some seven hundred people living in Cape Breton in the 1760s, about five hundred of them still at Louisbourg."[118]

The population of Cape Breton increased by about a third by the 1774 census which documented "532 settlers living in St. Peters, Isle Madame [far southeast coast of Cape Breton] and only 420 on the rest of Cape Breton."[119] Again, according to Morgan, although the British wanted to keep their friendship, the Mi'kmaq had no protections in the royal proclamation of 1763, and some dispersed to Newfoundland and St. Pierre and Miquelon. According to a 1774 census, "there were only 23 natives on Cape Breton Island."[120] And the records of 1785 show large quantities of fish still being exported from Gabarus Bay and other places along the coast.[121]

As noted, colonial surveyor Samuel Holland [1728-1801], under the command of Brigadier General James Wolfe, surveyed the area around Louisbourg and ultimately completed the most thorough official survey of the Cape Breton Island. He claimed that the fishing industry in Cape Breton "had employed 20,000 French before 1758."[122]

The American War for Independence which ended in 1783 scattered the United Empire Loyalists (UEL) and disbanded soldiers from the thirteen colonies to throughout the maritime region. At the time the British assumed control of the island, many of these settlers were moved from New England and other points south into Nova Scotia and what is now New Brunswick.[123] This was the case with Mrs. Gray's 4th great-grandfather Armstrong, an ancestor who made her a distant cousin of American astronaut Neil Armstrong, the first man on the moon. The settlement of Loyalists in Cape Breton was led by Abraham Cuyler, a former mayor of Albany, New York. The Loyalists were each given free land grants in Cape Breton, and Cuyler was given a good paying job as the secretary of the new colony.[124] According to Morgan, it is hard to accurately estimate the number of Loyalists who came to Cape Breton but "it seems that less than 500 came to the colony."[125]

19th and 20th Century Developments

In earlier days Gabarus was described as "a very lively place and all of the inhabitants obtained a living either directly or indirectly from the sea."[126] Over most of the 19th century in Cape Breton and in coastal villages like Gabarus, there was continuous growth in fishing and shipbuilding commerce.

According to the Laverys, the economy of the three Maritime colonies were relatively stable during the first half of the nineteenth century. Their fishing and lumbering industries were strong. "They sent fish to the West Indies, square timber to Great Britain, and sawn lumber to the U.S. To facilitate this trade, a shipbuilding industry arose, resulting in a unified integrated economy."[127]

In the late 1800s, trade was very brisk around Cape Breton Island with fish being shipped from the outports like Gabarus.

In Gabarus-born Lottie Morrison's interview with Ronald Caplan in 1985 about her early family history, she said that at that time [which we understood to be late 1800s] there were about 80 fishing boats in Gabarus and 18 sailing vessels, "all manned by Gabarus people." [128]

Down through the years a "great many small fishing schooners and later motorboats were built to carry out the shore fisheries and lobstering."[129] John Parker, the author of Cape Breton: Ships and Men, documented seven vessels that were built in Gabarus before 1900 including the "Elizabeth, Elizabeth Ryan, Matilda Hopewell, Robert Noble, Charles Valentine, E.M.G. Hardy, A.H. Hardy."[130] In addition to Captain John Grant, Mildred Grant's grandfather, Parker notes other prominent seamen of that time: "Isiah Mac Donald, John McDonald, A.N. Bagnell, Wesley Nichol, Phil Cann, and one whole family of sailors, Captains John, Robert, Herbert, E.E., and James Ormiston."[131]

Not all of the ships' captains in the 18th and 19th century were certified masters. The "'old sailors did not know celestial navigation; they got their latitude by noon sighting of the sun, and dead reckoning."[132] Many were self-taught and yet remarkably brave and successful.

By 1910 there were fewer sail-powered boats, and boats powered by gasoline engines were starting to dominate. The Laverys report that "Norman Hutt from Owl's Head in Gabarus Bay built gas-powered Cape Island boats about 28' long, which are still in use by fishermen today."[133]

Before he retired in 1902 and settled down to help his father run the family store, Mildred Gray's grandfather Captain John Grant voyaged with one of his two-masted cargo schooners laden with fish, tin for the lobster factories, timber, coal and other commodities. As was the case with Captain Grant, many men who owned vessels would have their eldest son as a first mate.

In 1903 Nova Scotia writer C.W. Vernon described a very healthy fishing industry in Cape Breton County at the beginning of the 20th century. That most certainly included Gabarus where, by 1901, there were "25 vessels, 560 boats and 1,284 men dependent upon the fishery for a living."[134] At the time, Gabarus was a major town, mostly because of the lobster factories.

At its peak during the early 1900s the Gabarus area had a population of more than 3,000 people and maintained 3 schools, 4 churches, 4 large stores and 5 lobster canneries."[135] Nearby Gull Cove, a few miles/km south of Gabarus village, must have been included in this description of the Gabarus area, since "from 1860 to the end of the First World War, Gull Cove was a thriving community."[136]

Shortly after the turn of the century, there was a significant shift in the weather, commerce, and population. According to the Annual Report of the Department of Marine and Fisheries in 1906 "…during prevailing high winds, lobsters became scarce…it did not pay either packer or fishermen to continue to the end, and the canneries were closed down."[137]

This added to the convergence of changes in economic opportunities at the Sydney steel plant that opened in 1901. This was the beginning of a huge shift in population. By the middle of the 20th century, the early prosperity of Gabarus from cod fishing and sailing ships had "declined to a stable group of fishermen/farmers, small business people, nurses and teachers."[138]

Now, the population is much smaller but is showing signs of renewal. Based on the 2011 census, Greater Gabarus has a population of 183 which is 25.3 percent higher than in 2001. This reflects a higher growth rate than Nova Scotia as a whole which is 1.5 percent higher than in 2001. The increase in Gabarus's population contrasts with a 4.7 percent decrease in the overall population of Cape Breton since the last census in 2006.[139]

Why is Gabarus growing while other places in Cape Breton are losing population? The location itself is one explanation. As Friends of Gabarus leader Tim Menk says: "How many picturesque fishing villages, with relatively intact old housing stock, have a great Bay of the Atlantic as the front yard and 10,000 acres of wilderness area as a backyard and also happen to be located on a dead-end Provincial road?"[140] Surely, Gabarus's 300-year history contributes to its uniqueness. Demographics play a big role too, as people are coming home after careers "away", and others, including retirees, are also attracted by its beauty, peace, and the character of community life. Gabarus is still a small community, but it is clearly experiencing healthy growth.

Barachois

Barachois is a word that needs to be explained. Mrs. Gray uses it frequently to refer to what other, non-Cape Bretoners, would call areas of the Gabarus Harbour. The "barachois" of Gabarus also refers to the village area, just up from Gabarus Beach on the Atlantic Ocean, where Highway 327 ends.

The word barachois seems to be unique to Cape Breton and Newfoundland, and it has its origins in the early Basque explorers and fishermen. The term barachois comes from a Basque word, "barratxoa", meaning "little bar."[141]

According to Thomas Pinchon, secretary to Governor Raymond of Louisbourg, from his memoirs published in 1760:

> *"they give the name barachois in this country to small ponds near the sea, from which they are separated only by a kind of causeway. There is no possibility of traveling even the distance of a league[142] along the coast without meeting with some of these pieces of water."*[143]

Other historians have also described the nature of the geographic setting. The "surface of the country [behind the bay] is very uneven, consisting for the most part of hills, rocks, woods, barrens, and a picturesque chain of upwards of forty fresh water lakes of various forms and sizes."[144]

Maps and direct personal observations of the Gabarus area show these lakes very close to the ocean. You can see Lever Lake to the west of Gabarus Village, Little Lake just off Gabarus Beach, Harris Lake past the Lakeview Cemetery and many others just off what Mrs. Gray and her neighbors call "outside beaches" on the east and south side of what is now the Gabarus Wilderness.

Scottish Settlers

The fundamental character of Gabarus and Cape Breton Island was strongly influenced by the settlement of the Scottish emigrants pouring out of Scotland's highlands and western islands. Their great numbers caused "a major change in the population of Cape Breton and ultimately set the tone for the island."[145]

In 1773 the ship Hector landed at Pictou, on the Nova Scotia mainland. Over the next few years boatloads of Scots arrived, and many settled in Cape Breton where they could own land. There were early settlements in Judique, River Inhabitants, and Mabou. In August 1802, a 245 ton ship, Northern Friends, sailed into Sydney Harbour, direct from Scotland. There were 415 Scots aboard who had heard that good land was available.[146] The new settlers were given land near Mira and Sydney, and by September were already clearing land. Many were from the Hebrides Islands off Western Scotland as were Mildred Gray's ancestors. These new settlers "fearlessly took their destiny into their own hands."[147] Early Scots settlers built log homes on stone foundations much like the one that Mrs. Gray's great-grandfather built in Grant's Hills.[148] The needs of the Highland settlers were different from, and perhaps more acute than, those of the Loyalists and others coming later from Britain, since they could bring little with them in the way of provisions or clothing to help them endure their first winter in Cape Breton. The Scottish settlers had to "learn building skills on the spot."[149] They had to be even more hardy and industrious to survive.

The migration was extraordinary. Between "1802 and 1845 at least 30,000 Scots came to settle on Cape Breton generally living on 200 acre grants for farming."[150] Some land grants were smaller, and some were larger. According to T.C. Haliburton the Scots were arriving each year by one or two thousand.[151]

Famine struck Cape Breton Island in 1816 when snow fell in June, and "the cold weather caused by the 1815 eruption of Mount Tambora in Indonesia that caused the sun to be blocked by ash."[152] But the Scottish settlers kept coming.

The "migration reached a peak between 1817 and 1820; the flow continued, and the last arrivals came around 1850."[153] In 1832 alone, "300 settlers from South Uist arrived in the backlands of East Bay, Catalone, Hillside, and Gabarus Lake."[154] Population numbers increased almost four-fold in less than 20 years; an estimate would put the "population of Cape Breton at 10,000 in 1820 and 37,278 in 1838."[155]

There was another great famine that began in 1845 with potato blight caused by infected potatoes that the settlers had brought from Ireland and Scotland. The famine lasted from 1845-1851.[156] At first the settlers thought they could feed the infected potatoes to their cattle, but the animals died. "This potato blight affected virtually the whole island."[157] The Mira River area was particularly affected, although historians point out that "it would have been worse if they had not "foraged berries, hunted wildlife, shared food or fished." [158] The years of famine brought an end of large-scale immigration to Cape Breton.[159] In 1850, the provincial government "declared that anyone possessing a crown lease in Cape Breton would henceforth own the land."[160] The Scots living along the water, like Mrs. Gray's ancestors, "fished, built ships, and cut timber for lumber. A simple but self-sufficient existence was carved from the island's resources."[161]

In Cape Breton communities there was, and still is, an ethos of communitarian support. In times of trouble merchants would extend credit, and "it was unheard of for a merchant to refuse goods on credit, no matter how poor he was or how impossible the prospect of payment."[162] This is wholly consistent with what Mildred Gray tells us about her grandfather and father and the Grant Store in Gabarus.

The 1818 and 1828 census data begins to show the influx of the Scots and Loyalists into Gabarus. Census taking in the Gabarus area documented the turning point in the heritage of the population in 1818 and 1828 when the census documented English, Irish and Scots named Armstrong, Ayles, Stacey, Turner, Hardy, Bagnell, Cann, Mann and MacGillivary. By the census of 1871 other Gabarus family names also included McDonald, McLeod, Slattery, Ormiston, Townsend, Gillis, and Harris.[163]

Methodism in Gabarus

Methodism arrived in Nova Scotia in the 1770s with the Loyalist settlers.[164] Although there were Catholic missionaries and priests in Cape Breton well before 1819, according to historian Robert J. Morgan, Gabarus had "never been visited by a minister of any religion when [Anglican] Rector Hibbert Binney visited in 1819 and baptized 62 people there."[165]

George and Mary Lavery in Tides and Times noted that, "the real strength of Methodism in the colonies lay not in the importation of ordained clergy, but in the spontaneous response of pioneer laymen to the religious needs of the communities."[166] This was the case with William Charlton who preached in Gabarus. As Mrs. Gray reports, in 1805 he married Ann Townsend of Louisbourg. They moved to Boston after their marriage, and he became a Methodist after a conversion experience there in 1816. Charlton was determined to return to Gabarus, and he became a prime mover in revivals starting in 1826. His service as the local Methodist preacher continued until his death in 1838. A marble tablet recognizing him was posted on the wall of the Gabarus United [Methodist] Church.[167] This was a time during which the roots of Methodism were laid down across Cape Breton.

Construction of the Methodist Church in Gabarus began in 1858 on land donated by James Bagnell.[168] But the congregation had existed since at least 1826 [the year the revivals started], since 1976 was the 150th anniversary of the Gabarus [Methodist] congregation.[169] The Methodist Church at Gabarus, known as the "Harbour Church", was finished and dedicated on January 2, 1867.[170] As Mrs. Gray describes, the church was the center of community life with numerous ongoing religious and social activities.

People invested time, money and effort in securing and maintaining and always improving the building. Church records show that in 1903 the Gabarus people purchased a McShane [church] bell costing $130. [171] This would have been a large expense at the time to which most members of the congregation would have contributed. Then "in 1913-1916 they added a chancel" to the church where the organist and the choir room were located.[172]

Mrs. Gray's description of her experience in the church confirms that Gabarus United was a very engaged and active congregation "with a continued interest in the world beyond its bounds."[173]

According to Mrs. Gray, in 1997 the Gabarus United Methodist Church was desanctified and sold to a private citizen. In 2001, the church was moved onto a new property across the street where it was placed on a new foundation. Following the death of the new owner, the property was sold again in 2006 to individuals who plan to restore it as a mixed-use public space. Their vision is to restore the historic church as a performance space, art gallery, and future home for a Gabarus Historical Society and the proposed Isle-Land Centre for the Public Interest.

Sydney Steel Plant and Gabarus Wilderness Area

When the Sydney steel plant opened in 1901 many people moved into Sydney for the jobs. As Mrs. Gray points out, this caused substantial decrease in the population of Gabarus, Gull Cove and the whole area. As Mrs. Gray tells us, she and her husband Duncan both worked at the steel plant for a period of time.

The steel plant was a large regional employer until 1967 when the announcement was made that it would shut down in April 1968. The Nova Scotia government moved to buy the plant and make it a provincial crown corporation. At the same time, a federal agency, Cape Breton Development Corporation (DEVCO), was formed to address the need for industrial development in Cape Breton.

According to the Laverys in Tides and Times, around 1972, DEVCO "started to recommend that the Nova Scotia government acquire land in the Gabarus area for possible expansion in the future."[174] At that time, the government leaders identified the Gabarus area as "one of the last possible sites for industrial expansion, with its excellent deep water harbour and proximity to a large labor pool in Sydney."[175] They even talked about building 4-lane highway connecting Sydney and Gabarus.

On July 27th, 1974 the Cape Breton Post featured an article that described how "4,000 acres around Gabarus Bay had been expropriated by the provincial government."[176] Mrs. Gray mentions that as a result of the expropriation, families of the early settlers who held title to the land received small payments. The province "acquired an additional 3,000 acres, all the land to the south and east of Gabarus, all the way to Belfry Gut."[177] The proposed industrial development never took place, and now this area is designated as the Gabarus Wilderness Area comprising a total of 9,254 acres.[178]

Center of the 20th Century Communications Revolution

Cape Breton has been a center of 20th century developments in modern communication with key points in the communities of Baddeck, Glace Bay, and Gabarus.

Alexander Graham Bell (1847–1922), the inventor of the first practical telephone, and his wife Mabel spent the last thirty-seven years of their lives between their estate in Baddeck, Beinn Bhreagh ("beautiful mountain" in Gaelic), and their home in Washington,. D.C. When Dr. Bell visited Cape Breton for the first time he famously exclaimed: "*I have travelled around the globe. I have seen the Canadian and American Rockies, the Andes, the Alps and the Highlands of Scotland, but for simple beauty, Cape Breton outrivals them all.*"[179]

The Bells' home was built overlooking the Bras d'Or Lake on 600 acres of land that took them seven years to acquire in the late 1880s from a number of landowners.[180] Dr. Bell and his wife Mabel are both buried on their estate.

Dr. Bell's impact was wide ranging, in his lifetime and beyond. The greatness of his contributions was recognized at his death when at the end of Bell's funeral,

> *every phone on the continent of North America was silenced in honor of the man who had given to mankind the means for direct communication at a distance.* [181]

In addition to Dr. Bell's significant contributions to science, a colleague who knew him well wrote that "The fact that he never spoke disparagingly of others was a remarkable trait, the value of which nowadays I appreciate more than I did when he was alive." [182]

Before he died in 1922, Dr. Bell was able to witness the accomplishment of his fellow inventor Guglielmo Marconi, also set in Cape Breton.

> *The new world's home of wireless is Cape Breton, for it was here that Marconi came and made a reality of his dream of linking by wireless the New World with the Old.*[183]

The international wireless revolution started in Cape Breton when Italian inventor Guglielmo Marconi (1874–1937), sent a transmission from the Marconi station at Table Head in Glace Bay on 14 December 1902. This became the first radio message to cross the Atlantic from North America.

Marconi was another intriguing historic figure. Eric Larson's engaging book *Thunderstruck* tells a tale of Marconi family lore that soon after his birth an elderly gardener commented on the size of his ears: "Che orecchi grandi ha!" His mother responded, "He will be able to hear the still, small voice of the air."[184]

Marconi's tutors and private lessons included lessons on electricity by a leading professor in Livorno. At that time Marconi was also "introduced to a retired telegrapher, Nello Marchetti, who was losing his eyesight." Through their friendship and time together, "Marchetti taught Marconi Morse Code and techniques for sending messages by telegraph."[185]

Marconi inherited more than blue eyes from his Irish mother. Although he had virtually no formal schooling in his childhood, his mother taught him English, and he spoke it flawlessly.[186] His perfect English may have contributed to his effectiveness in working with his Cape Breton admirers like Alex. Johnson, a newspaperman at the Sydney *Record*[187] to secure the location and funding to make his test transmission. Dominion Coal Company provided the location, Table Head in Glace Bay, and the Canadian government of Prime Minister Sir Wilfrid Laurier contributed $80,000. A powerful Nova Scotia politician, Hon.

William S. Fielding, who was minister of finance, was one of the leaders who saw the value of Marconi's experiment. Marconi, who was only twenty-eight years old at the time of the first transatlantic wireless transmission, secured a contract with the Cunard Steamship Company, and they started regular wireless ship-to-shore communication. Marconi was one of the fortunate people who missed taking the Titanic's maiden voyage in 1912, but ship-to shore wireless is credited with saving the lives of 712 of the 2,000 passengers on board from that disaster.[188]

At the time the British Empire "controlled one quarter of the world's population and one quarter of its land."[189] Within a few years of that first transmission, all the member states of the British Empire were linked by Marconi stations.[190]

The central telegraph office in Gabarus was established in 1902, the same year as Marconi's transmission. For many years the Gabarus area telegraph communication was the main method of conducting business and keeping in touch with relatives in the United States and other parts of Canada. At that time, Gabarus was one of the most populous areas in Cape Breton, and Cape Breton was a "focal point for news gathering from all of North America and Europe."[191]

Morse Code became the language that connected coastal outports and villages. Gabarus was the site of the central telegraph office for 18 communities along the eastern coast of Cape Breton Island.

The actual telegraph workstation in Mrs. Gray's home took up a very small area, a few square feet next to her front door and close to the bottom of the stairs. One of Mrs. Gray's neighbors kept a scrapbook of all telegrams, and after her death, the family gave the scrapbook to Mrs. Gray. The messages on the green paper of the *Department of Transport Telecommunications Division* are short but expressive: "Mom better. Writing tonight. Love." and "Roads blocked. Can't get home. Love." and "Dad in Halifax. Due Government Wharf Sydney noon tomorrow Sunday. Love." The roads being blocked was a common issue, especially in winter, as "public snow removal did not really begin until the highways were paved in the early 1950s."[192]

Mrs. Gray would receive messages in Morse Code and then relay them by telephone to government-employed couriers in the other communities. Mildred Gray operated the telegraph and then the switchboard from her home twenty-four hours a day. She was always on call. Her home was communications central. When she was a telegraph operator starting in 1947, there were very few telephones, and she often had to deliver telegrams on foot. In 1959 the telegraph service in Gabarus was terminated, leaving only a few telephones and Louisbourg as the central telegraph for the area. When the telegraph office closed, she was praised by her employer, the Canadian Department of Transport: "We found Mrs. Gray to be an efficient, conscientious employee who was always willing to perform duties over and above."[193] This was her nature, to work hard and go beyond what was asked.

Then, in "May 1961 Maritime Tel and Tel began telephone service in Gabarus; 79 people subscribed to the service which extended to Gabarus Lake, Fourchu, Framboise, and Sterling."[194] Mrs. Gray was hired as the central switchboard operator.

Mrs. Gray was at the nexus of historic change in communications. When she retired in 1976, the event was the source of both local and provincial news. Since she served as the community's central operator for so many years, you might expect that news to be confined to Gabarus and its environs. In fact, Gabarus was the last community in Nova Scotia to be provided with modern dial telephone service. Her retirement heralded an important cultural change, from rural, crank telephones and their replacement by more efficient, but impersonal, dial phones. Privacy may have been suspect with the old system, and connections may not have always been the greatest, but there was a more lively sense of personal connection. As Mrs. Gray says in her recollections "Even though I was just the operator, there was a lot more to it." Like all change, it involved a tradeoff, in this case, privacy and efficiency for personal attention.

The Spelling of Gabarus

As we have discussed, the name of Gabarus is a very old one, named after the Cabarrus family. The "name is recorded in early maps with various spellings but always beginning with Gabu- or Gabo-."[195]

Tides and Times provides a comprehensive list of the many forms and spellings of the name Gabarus: "Chapeau Rouge, Gabor, Gabari, Gabori, Gabory, Cabarus, Gabarus, Gabbarus, Gabaron, Gaberus, Gabarous, and Gabarouse."[196] In most of the English accounts of the sieges of Louisbourg in 1745 and 1758 the name Gabarus appears as "Chapeau Rouge," but several historians think that the connection between the two names was because the "respective names sounded the same in ordinary conversation."[197] Although it was always called Gabori or Gabarus by the French, [Chapeau Rouge] "seems to have come from the 'little knowledge' of the 'linguisters' of the expedition [New Englanders] who would be more familiar with the spoken rather than the written word."[198]

Gabarus' Methodist Minister George Lavery's research into the spelling of the place name ultimately resulted in an official name change for the community, so that all maps, road signs and community signs would show the name spelled in the same way. In 1970, at a meeting of the Gabarus United Methodist Church it had been decided that the official spelling used by the church would be "Gabarus", not "Gabarouse."[199] Members of Gabarus United congregation decided to see if they could get the province to change all of the signs to the current spelling.

Mrs. Gray recalled that when the Tides and Times history of Gabarus was published in 1991 [by Mary and George Lavery], the spelling became consistently Gabarus after that. According to Mrs. Gray, the "Tides and Times Minister Lavery said that the correct spelling was 'us', so we stopped spelling it 'ouse'."

This section on the Highlights of Gabarus History is designed to inform a starting place for further study about the history of Gabarus. Sources cited in the bibliography can serve as a launching point for additional reading. Feel free to contact me at the www.zeitgeistwest.com website with comments, questions and suggestions.

The following facts and timeline may be helpful in reviewing the flow of historic developments in Cape Breton and Gabarus. Again, this is a brief outline, and there are more many more elements that could be added to paint a fuller picture of key events.

Year	Event
Before 986	Mi'kmaq native people and their ancestors are the only people living on Cape Breton
986 and 1000 A.D.	Norsemen Biarne Heriulfason in Leif Ericsson likely visited the southeastern coast of Cape Breton[200]
1372	Basque fishermen start coming to the cod- and whale-rich seas around Cape Breton[201]
1497	Giovanni and Sebastian Cabato first expedition and possible landfall in Cape Breton[202]
1716	Gabarus "Gabory": 1 habitant, 10 fishermen; 2 chaloupes* (First record of settlement at Gabarus)[203]
1745	First siege of Louisbourg
1752	Census of Gabarus settlement: 25 people including men and women, children and domestic "thirty-six" months men, and livestock, schooners and bateaux including Jeanne Beaudry, the first known female entrepreneur of Gabarus who employed three fishermen[204]
1758	Second siege of Louisbourg
1758	50 shallops in Gabarus; fishermen in Cape Breton = 15,138[205]
1763	Treaty of Paris signed on February 10th after Britain's victory over France and Spain. The signing of the treaty formally ended the French and Indian War.

1793	All of Cape Breton had 611 permanent residents.[206]
1805	Cape Breton government administrator A.C. Dodd reported sighting 1,500 caribou on the Gabarus barrens between Louisbourg and Gabarus[207]
1818	Gabarouse Bay census noted 22 men (and likely a near equal number of women) and 60 children.[208]
1871	Greater Gabarus's first official census of the new Dominion of Canada documented 153 families of English and Scottish descent; 1,743 people[209]
Before 1900	Seven schooners of up to 123 tons were built at Gabarus before 1900.[210]
	Gabarus exported via a fleet of 27 large schooners to the Caribbean, Europe, and Africa.[211]
1900	Over 3,000 people in the Gabarus area; three schools, five churches and four "large" stores[212]
	18 vessels operating out of Gabarus[213]
	Approximately 200 fishing boats operated out of Gabarus from March to December[214]
1902	Gabarus Telegraph Office opened
1947	Electricity in Gabarus
1955	Road to Gabarus paved
1977	Last Gabarus school closed[215]
1979	15 boats fishing for lobster crab and mackerel[216]
1990	One small store with gas pumps[217]
2011	Greater Gabarus has a population of 183 which is 25.3% higher than in 2001[218]
2013	9 boats fishing out of Gabarus[219]

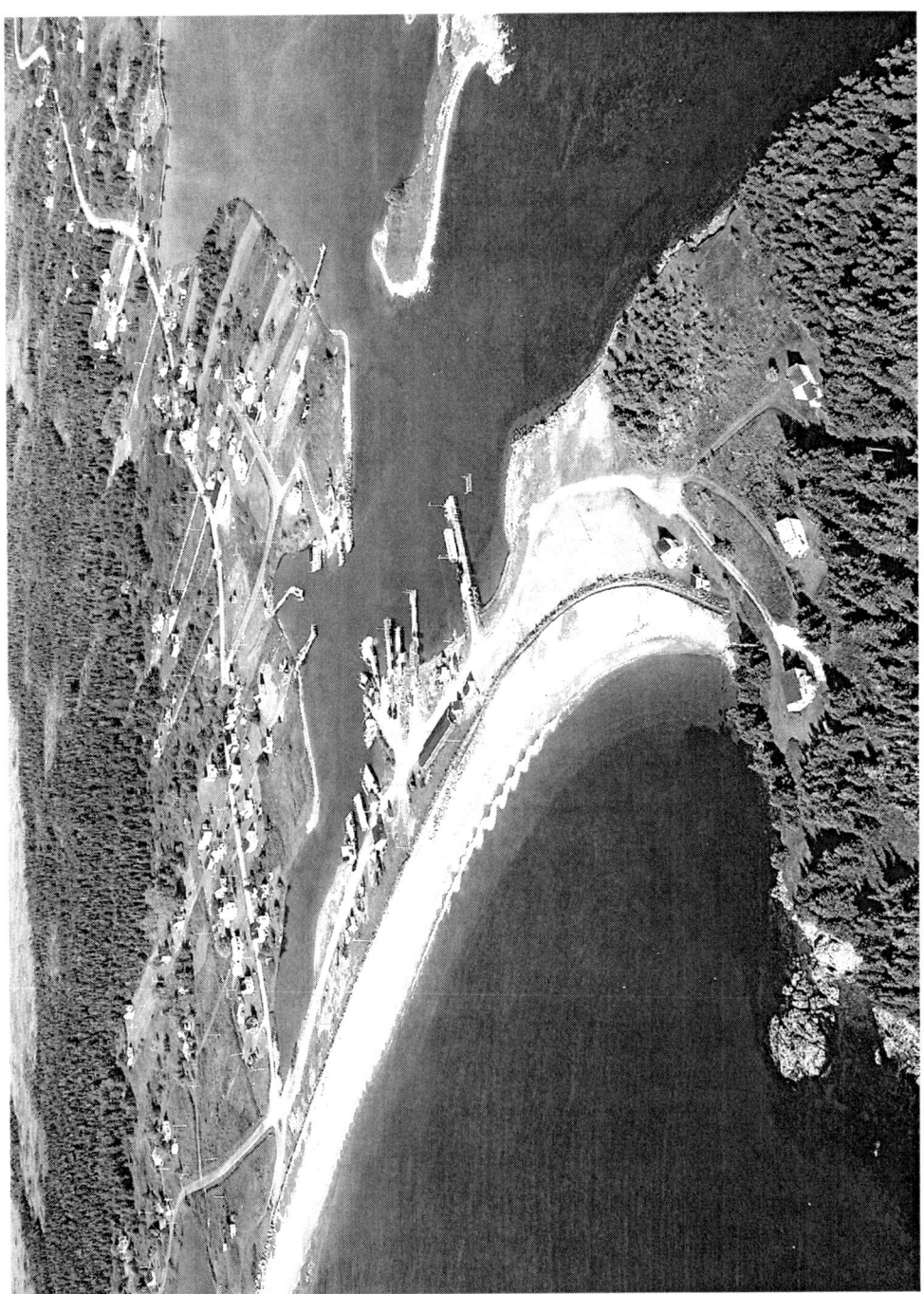

AERIAL PHOTOGRAPH OF GABARUS VILLAGE BY
WARREN GORDON PHOTOGRAPHIC
WWW.GORDONPHOTO.COM
USED WITH PERMISSION

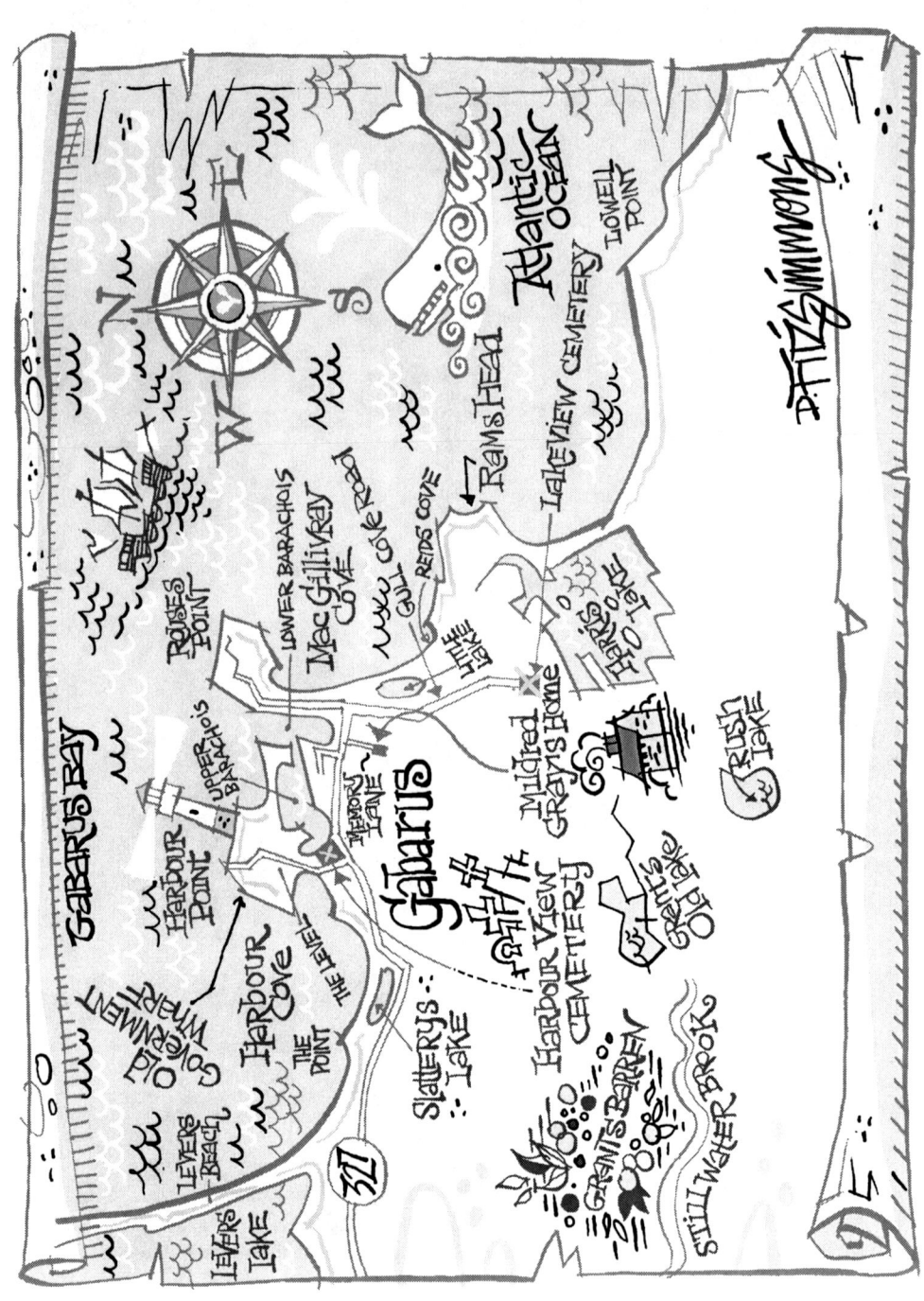

Drawing of Gabarus Village
by David "Fitz" Fitzsimmons
Used with permission

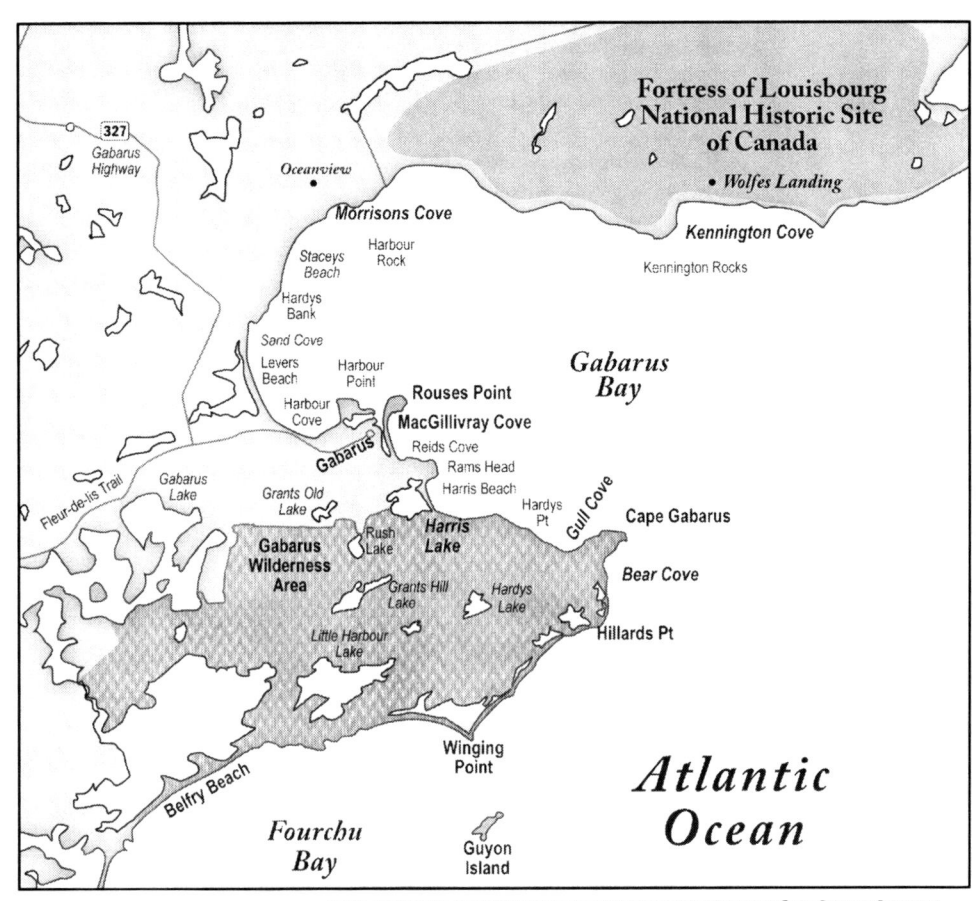

ALL PLACE NAMES ARE ACCURATE BASED ON CURRENT MAPS FROM CAPE BRETON REGIONAL MUNICIPALITY. THIS REDRAWN MAP IS ONLY GENERALLY ACCURATE AS TO DISTANCES. SCALE IS APPROXIMATELY 1"=2 MILES/3.22 KM. PLEASE USE OFFICIAL MAPS FOR NAVIGATION.

Highlights of Gabarus History   227

Endnotes

[1] Jane Taber. "For a Nova Scotia Fishing Village, There's Danger of Falling into the Ocean." The Globe and Mail, April 29, 2013.

[2] Mi'kmaq is the plural form of the singular Mi'kmaw, and when one uses the word Mi'kmaq it always refers to more than one Mi'kmaw person or the entire nation. The word Mi'kmaw can be adjectival. Simone Poliandri, First Nations, Identity, and Reserve Life: The Mi'kmaq of Nova Scotia (Lincoln: University of Nebraska Press, 2011), 275.

[3] "Tradition, Change and Survival: Mi'kmaq Tourist Art," McCord Museum of Canadian History, accessed July 7, 2013, http://www.mccord-museum.qc.ca/en/keys/webtours/tourID/VQ_P1_3_EN.

[4] Robert J. Morgan, Rise Again! The Story of Cape Breton Island, Book One (Wreck Cove: Breton Books, 2008), 2

[5] As quoted in Brian Douglas Tennyson, ed., Impressions of Cape Breton (Sydney: University College of Cape Breton Press, 1986), 265-266.

[6] Tennyson, Impressions, 229.

[7] Clary Croft, A Maritimer's Miscellany (Halifax: Nimbus Publishing, 2007), 17.

[8] The Micmacs prefer the phonetic spelling Mi'kmaq, "The Mi'kmaq, Cape Breton University: Mi'kmaq Resource Centre, accessed May 13, 2013, http://www.cbu.ca/mrc/the-mikmaq.

[9] "The Mi'kmaq."

[10] J.G. Bourinot, Historical and Descriptive Account of the Island of Cape Breton, and of its Memorials of the French Regime (Montreal: W. Foster Brown, 1892), 7.

[11] Ibid., 7.

[12] Morgan, Rise Again!, Book 1,14.

[13] T. Menk and E. Kersey, "Naming of Gabarus" (paper presented at the annual meeting for the Canadian Society for the Study of Names, Montreal, Quebec, May 30, 2010).

[14] Christopher Moore, Louisbourg Portraits: Five Dramatic True Tales of People Who Lived in an Eighteenth Century Garrison Town (Toronto: McClelland & Stewart Ltd., 1982), 113.

[15] Ibid., 114.

[16] Mark Kurlansky, Cod: A Biography of the Fish That Changed the World (New York: Penguin Books, 1997), 24.

[17] Moore, Louisbourg Portraits, 105.

[18] Kurlansky, Cod, 50.

[19] Morgan, Rise Again!, Book 1, 15.

[20] C. Bruce Fergusson, "John Cabot's Landfall, 1497: It WAS Cape Breton!," Cape Breton's Magazine 70 (June 1996), 54; and Charles Bruce Fergusson, "Cabot's Landfall," Dalhousie Review 33 (Winter 1953): 257-76.

[21] Morgan, Rise Again!, Book 1, 15.

[22] Peter Cumming, Heather MacLeod, and Linda Strachan, eds, The Story of Framboise: An Eachdraidh air Flambois (Framboise: St. Andrew's Presbyterian, 1984), 38.

[23] Kurlansky, Cod, 32.

[24] Ibid., 51.

[25] Moore, Louisbourg Portraits, 105.

[26] Ibid., 106.

[27] Ibid., 104.

[28] Morgan, Rise Again!, Book 1, 18.

[29] Ibid., 19.

[30] Ibid., 14.

[31] "The Mi'kmaq."

[32] M. Lavery, and G. Lavery, Tides and Times: Life on the Cape Breton Coast at Gabarus and Vicinity, 1713-1990 (Scarborough: Private Printer, 1991), 2.

[33] Morgan, Rise Again!, Book 1, 21.

[34] As quoted in C. Corbin et al., eds., Aspects of Louisbourg: Essays on the History of an 18th-Century French Community (Sydney: Cape Breton University Press, 1995), 198.

[35] Kurlansky, Cod, 34.

[36] Ibid., 45.

[37] Ibid.

[38] Kurlansky, Cod, 44.

[39] Ibid., 45.

[40] Ibid., 10.

[41] J.A. Hutchings, and R.A. Myers, "The Biological Collapse of Atlantic Cod Off Newfoundland and Labrador: An Exploration of Historical Changes in Exploitation, Harvesting Technology, and Management." In The North Atlantic Fishery: Strengths, Weaknesses, and Challenges, ed. R. Arnason et al. (Charlottetown, PEI: Institute of Island Studies University of Prince Edward Island, 1995), 39.

[42] Ibid., 81.

[43] Ibid., 82.

[44] Dan Bortolotti,"A Moratorium on Atlantic Cod Fishing Starts Showing Results." Canadian Geographic, December 2011, accessed July 10, 2013, http://www.canadiangeographic.ca/magazine/dec11/wildlife_cod.asp.

[45] Lopez, Barry. "The Whaleboat: It's Surprising How Far a Ten-inch Craft Can Carry You." Outside Magazine, May 1998; accessed July 14, 2013, http://www.outsideonline.com/outdoor-adventure/The-Whaleboat.html; and David Hackett Fischer, Champlain's Dream: The European Founding of North America (New York: Random House, 2008), 626.

[46] Herman Melville, Moby Dick; or, The White Whale (Boston: St. Botolph Society, 1892), 525.

[47] Moore, Louisbourg Portraits, 107; Fischer, Champlain's Dream, 625-626.

[48] S. J. Hornsby, Nineteenth-Century Cape Breton: A Historical Geography (Montreal: McGill-Queen's University Press, 1992), 8.

[49] Moore, Louisbourg Portraits, 105-108.

[50] Lavery, Tides and Times, 14.

[51] Ibid., 5.

[52] Moore, Louisbourg Portraits, 107.

[53] Morgan, Rise Again!, Book 1, 134.

[54] Ibid., 16.

[55] Morgan, Rise Again!, Book 1, 16; and Lavery, Tides and Times, 1.

[56] Morgan, Rise Again!, Book 1, 16; and Moore, Louisbourg Portraits, 114.

[57] Menk and Kersey, "Naming of Gabarus."

[58] "Les Cabarrus," Cote Sud Memoire, accessed March 18, 2013, http://www.cotesudmemoirevive.com/templates/cotesudmemoirevive.php?id_page=45.

[59] "Les Cabarrus."

[60] "Les Cabarrus."

[61] Joseph LeHuenen, "The Role of the Basque, Breton and Norman Cod Fishermen in the Discovery of North America from the XVIth to the End of the XVIIIth Century," Arctic 37 (December 1984): 520-527; Edouard Ducéré, Recherches Historiques Sur La Peche De La Morue Et La Decouverte De Terre-Neuve (Unknown: J. Emperauger, 1893), accessed May 29, 2013, http://books.google.ca/books?id=q-h5AAAAM AAJ&pg=PA28&dq=baleines+ducere+capbreton&hl=en&sa=X&ei=_rgCUuaWFsHwigL1-YHgCw&redir_esc=y#v=onepage&q=baleines%20 ducere%20capbreton&f=false; Menk and Kersey, "Naming of Gabarus," 213-214; and Aegidius Fauteux, "La Baie de Cabarrus." Bulletin des Recherches Historiques 35 (February 1929): 72-74.

[62] "Les Cabarrus."

[63] Menk and Kersey, "Naming of Gabarus."

[64] Lavery, Tides and Times, 12.

[65] Not publicly accessible since the establishment of Fortress Louisbourg as a National Historic Site.

[66] United States, Navy Department, Hydrographic Office, Nova Scotia Pilot: Bay of Fundy, Southeast Coast of Nova Scotia and Coast of Cape Breton Island (Washington: U.S. Government Printing Office, 1918), accessed March 8, 2013, http://books.google.com/books?id=Vm0DAAAAYAAJ &pg=PA430&dq=temperate+industrious+and+thriving+people+gabaru s&hl=en&sa=X&ei=F8_cUYucHOKrigLu9IDYDQ&ved=0CDUQ6AE wAQ#v=onepage&q=temperate%20industrious%20and%20thriving%20 people%20gabarus&f=false.

[67] Robert J. Morgan, Early Cape Breton: From Founding to Famine (Wreck Cove: Breton Books, 2000), 83.

[68] Charles William Vernon, Cape Breton, Canada (Toronto: Nation Publishing Company, 1903), 283.

[69] Lavery, Tides and Times, 14.

[70] Ibid., 115.

[71] Vernon, Cape Breton, 283.

[72] Lavery, Tides and Times, 117.

[73] Navy Department, Nova Scotia Pilot.

[74] Morgan, Rise Again!, Book 1, 32.

[75] Corbin et al., eds., Aspects of Louisbourg, 4.

[76] Clara Dennis, Cape Breton Over (Toronto: The Ryerson Press, 1942), 119.

[77] Corbin et al., eds., Aspects of Louisbourg, 3.

[78] Ibid., 10.

[79] Moore, Louisbourg Portraits, 7.

[80] Lavery, Tides and Times, 2.

[81] As quoted in Corbin et al., eds., Aspects of Louisbourg, 228.

[82] As quoted in Corbin et al., eds., Aspects of Louisbourg, 199.

[83] As quoted in Corbin et al., eds., Aspects of Louisbourg, 198.

[84] As quoted in Corbin et al., eds., Aspects of Louisbourg, 230.

[85] John P. Parker, Cape Breton Ships and Men (London: George J. McLeod Limited, 1967), 137.

[86] As quoted in Corbin et al., eds., Aspects of Louisbourg, 206-207.

[87] Morgan, Rise Again!, Book 1, 43.

[88] Morgan, Rise Again!, Book 1, 47; and Lavery, Tides and Times, 9.

[89] Morgan, Rise Again!, Book 1, 46; and Lavery, Tides and Times, 9.

[90] Lavery, Tides and Times, 11.

[91] Francis Parkman, A Half Century of Conflict, France and England in North America, Volume II (Boston: Little, Brown, and Company, 1897), 109.

[92] Morgan, Rise Again!, Book 1, 47.

[93] Ibid.

[94] Morgan, Rise Again!, Book 1, 48.

[95] Morgan, Rise Again!, Book 1, 49; and Corbin et al., eds., Aspects of Louisbourg, 11.

[96] Morgan, Rise Again!, Book 1, 49.

[97] P. Lotz, and J. Lotz, Cape Breton Island (Vancouver: Douglas, David, and Charles, 1974), 47.

[98] Dennis, Cape Breton Over, 130.

[99] P. Lotz, and J. Lotz, Cape Breton Island (Vancouver: Douglas, David, and Charles, 1974), 47.

[100] Morgan, Rise Again!, Book 1, 50.

[101] Acadian Home, "1752 Census of Île Royale by Le Sieur De La Roque," S.E. Dawson, 1906, Transcribed Maureen McNeil, accessed January 21, 2013, http://www.acadian-home.org/1752laroque.pdf.

[102] As quoted in Corbin et al., eds., Aspects of Louisbourg, 12.

[103] Morgan, Rise Again!, Book 1, 51.

[104] J.S. McLennan, Louisbourg From Its Foundation To Its Fall, 1713-1758 (Halifax: The Book Room Limited, 1990), 245.

[105] Dennis, Cape Breton Over, 133.

[106] Leslye Choyce, Nova Scotia Shaped by the Sea: A Living History (Toronto: Penguin Group, 1996), 115.

[107] Lavery, Tides and Times, 23.

[108] Corbin et al., eds., Aspects of Louisbourg, 296.

[109] Lavery, Tides and Times, 23.

[110] Corbin et al., eds., Aspects of Louisbourg, 293.

[111] J. Witham, "Grant Family Tree," Personal Communication, July 1, 2013.

[112] Ibid.

[113] Ibid.

[114] Morgan, Rise Again!, Book 1, 52.

[115] Ibid., 57.

[116] Ibid., 52.

[117] Lavery, Tides and Times, 23.

[118] Brian Douglas Tennyson, ed., Impressions of Cape Breton (Sydney: University College of Cape Breton Press, 1986), xiii.

[119] Morgan, Rise Again!, Book 1, 59.

[120] Ibid., 56.

[121] Lavery, Tides and Times, 31.

[122] Morgan, Rise Again!, Book 1, 69.

[123] Ibid., 2.

[124] Ibid., 65.

[125] Ibid., 68.

[126] Parker, Cape Breton Ships, 138.

[127] Lavery, Tides and Times, 52-53.

[128] Ronald Caplan, ed., "With Lottie Morrison from Gabarus," Cape Breton's Magazine 40 (August 1985): 1-10, accessed February 13, 2013, http://capebretonsmagazine.com/modules/publisher/item.php?itemid=1935.

[129] Parker, Cape Breton Ships, 138.

[130] Ibid.

[131] Ibid.

[132] Lavery, Tides and Times, 99.

[133] Ibid., 100.

[134] Ibid., 83.

[135] Ibid.

[136] Ibid., 2.

[137] Canada, Department of Marine and Fisheries, 39th Annual Report of the Department of Marine and Fisheries, Seasonal Paper No. 22 (Ottawa: Government Printer, 1906), 37.

[138] Lavery, Tides and Times, 136.

[139] Nova Scotia Community Counts, "Census of Population 2001, 2006, and 2011," accessed April 7, 2013, http://www.gov.ns.ca/finance/communitycounts/profiles/community/default.asp?gnum=com1722&gview=2&glevel=com.

[140] Tim Menk, "Reasons for Gabarus' Population Growth," e-mail message to author, September 2, 2013.

[141] Patrice Brasseur, Dictionnaire des Régionalismes du Français de Terre-Neuve (Tübingen: Niemeyer, 2001), 41.

[142] A league originally referred to the distance a person could walk in an hour, approximately 3.5 miles/5.6 km. "A League," Unit Conversion, accessed April 14, 2013, http://www.unitconversion.org/length/league-conversion.html%20accessed%20on%20april%2014.

[143] Tennyson, Impressions, 15.

[144] Lavery, Tides and Times, 51.

[145] Morgan, Rise Again!, Book 1, 112.

[146] Lavery, Tides and Times, 33.

[147] Morgan, Early Cape Breton, 85-86.

[148] Morgan, Rise Again!, Book 1, 114.

[149] Lavery, Tides and Times, 46.

[150] Morgan, Early Cape Breton, 55.

[151] Tennyson, Impressions, xiii.

[152] Ibid., 92.

[153] Morgan, Rise Again!, Book 1, 82.

[154] Ibid., 117.

[155] Ibid., 118.

[156] Ibid., 121.

[157] Morgan, Early Cape Breton, 139.

[158] Ibid., 144.

[159] Ibid., 149.

[160] Morgan, Rise Again!, Book 1, 130.

[161] Ibid., 83.

[162] Morgan, Early Cape Breton, 147.

[163] Lavery, Tides and Times, 35-36, 65.

[164] Ibid., 38.

[165] Morgan, Early Cape Breton, 71-72.

[166] Lavery, Tides and Times, 39.

[167] Ibid., 40.

[168] Ibid., 42-44.

[169] Ibid., 149.

[170] Ibid., 52.

[171] Ibid., 91.

[172] Ibid., 118.

[173] Ibid., 125.

[174] Ibid., 144-145.

[175] Ibid.

[176] Ibid.

[177] Ibid.

[178] "Gabarus Wilderness Area," Wikimapia, accessed March 23, 2013, http://wikimapia.org/9852354/Gabarus-Wilderness-Area.

[179] Croft, Miscellany, 151.

[180] Dennis, Cape Breton Over, 207.

[181] Harold S. Osborne, Biographical Memoir of Alexander Graham Bell: 1847-1922, Vol. XXIII (Washington: Literary Licensing, 1943), accessed February 28, 2013, http://books.nap.edu/html/biomems/abell.pdf.

[182] Ibid., 19.

[183] Dennis, Cape Breton Over, 103.

[184] Eric Larson, Thunderstruck (New York: Crown Publishing, 2006), 16.

[185] Ibid., 19.

[186] Ibid.,18.

[187] Dennis, Cape Breton Over, 104.

[188] Ibid., 107.

[189] Larson, Thunderstruck, 52.

[190] "Marconi National Historic Site of Canada," Parks Canada, accessed

February 16, 2013, http://www.pc.gc.ca/eng/lhn-nhs/ns/marconi/natcul.aspx.

[191] Lavery, Tides and Times, 121.

[192] Tennyson, Impressions, xxi.

[193] Mildred Gray, "Personal Correspondence from Canadian Department of Transport." Personal Communication, July 1, 2013.

[194] Lavery, Tides and Times, 122.

[195] Ibid., 2.

[196] Ibid., 161-162.

[197] Bourinot, Historical and Descriptive Account, 98-99.

[198] McLennan, Louisbourg From Its Foundation, 138.

[199] Lavery, Tides and Times, 148.

[200] Bourinot, Historical and Descriptive Account, 7.

[201] Historian Edouard Ducéré indicated that around 1372 the Basques were hunting whales in the New World and entered the mouth of the Bay of Saint Lawrence. See Edouard Ducéré, Dictionnaire Historique de Bayonne (Bayonne: Foltzer, 1911); and Menk and Kersey, "Naming of Gabarus."

[202] Fergusson, "John Cabot's Landfall," 257-76.

[203] Lavery, Tides and Times, 3.

[204] Ibid., 13.

[205] Ibid., 15.

[206] Lavery, Tides and Times, 32.

[207] Morgan, Early Cape Breton, 83.

[208] Lavery, Tides and Times, 36.

[209] Lavery, Tides and Times, 71.

[210] Ibid., 136.

[211] Ibid., 136.

[212] Ibid.

[213] Caplan, "With Lottie Morrison," 2.

[214] Morgan, Rise Again!, Book 1, 136.

[215] Lavery, Tides and Times, 137.

[216] Ibid., 149.

[217] Ibid., 152.

[218] Nova Scotia Community Counts, "Census of Population 2001, 2006, and 2011."

[219] Kenneth Sherwood, "Number of Boats Fishing Out of Gabarus." Personal Communication, August 27, 2013.

Select Bibliography for Highlights of Gabarus History

Acadian Home. "1752 Census of Ile Royale by Le Sieur De La Roque." S.E. Dawson, 1906. Transcribed Maureen McNeil. Accessed January 21, 2013. http://www.acadian-home.org/1752laroque.pdf.

Bortolotti, Dan. "A Moratorium on Atlantic Cod Fishing Starts Showing Results." Canadian Geographic, December 2011. Accessed July 10, 2013. http://www.canadiangeographic.ca/magazine/dec11/wildlife_cod.asp.

Bourinot, J. G. Historical and Descriptive Account of the Island of Cape Breton, and of its Memorials of the French Regime. Montreal: W. Foster Brown, 1892.

Brasseur, Patrice. Dictionnaire des Régionalismes du Français de Terre-Neuve. Tübingen: Niemeyer, 2001.

Brown, Thomas J. "Place Names of the Province of Nova Scotia: 1922." Accessed March 26, 2013. http://archive.org/stream/placenamesofprov00browrich/placenamesofprov00browrich_djvu.txt.

Campey, Lucille H. After the Hector: The Scottish Pioneers of Nova Scotia and Cape Breton 1773- 1852. Toronto: Natural Heritage Books, 2007.

Canada. Department of Marine and Fisheries. 39th Annual Report of the Department of Marine and Fisheries. Seasonal Paper No. 22. Ottawa: Government Printer, 1906.

Cape Breton Gen Web Project. "Index to 1811 and 1818 Census Rolls." Accessed April 14, 2013. http://www.capebretongenweb.com/censindx.html.

Cape Breton University: Mi'kmaq Resource Centre. "The Mi'kmaq." Accessed May 13, 2013. http://www.cbu.ca/mrc/the-mikmaq.

Caplan, Ronald, ed. "With Lottie Morrison from Gabarus." Cape Breton's Magazine 40 (August 1985): 1-10. Accessed February 13, 2013. http://capebretonsmagazine.com/modules/publisher/item.php?itemid=1935.

Choyce, Leslye. Nova Scotia Shaped by the Sea: A Living History. Toronto: Penguin Group, 1996.

Corbin, C., Krause, E., and W. O'Shea, eds. Aspects of Louisbourg: Essays on the History of an 18th-Century French Community. Sydney: Cape Breton University Press, 1995.

Cote Sud Memoire Vive. "Les Cabarrus." Accessed March 18, 2013. http://www.cotesudmemoirevive.com/templates/cotesudmemoirevive.php?id_page=45.

Cote Sud Memoire Vive. "100 Ans Avant Christophe Colomb." Accessed May 13, 2013. http://www.cotesudmemoirevive.com/templates/cotesudmemoirevive.php?id_page=66.

Croft, Clary. A Maritimer's Miscellany. Halifax: Nimbus Publishing, 2007.

Cumming, Peter, Heather MacLeod, and Linda Strachan, eds. The Story of Framboise: An Eachdraidh air Flambois. Framboise: St. Andrew's Presbyterian, 1984.

Dennis, Clara. Cape Breton Over. Toronto: The Ryerson Press, 1942.

Dennis, Clara. Down in Nova Scotia. My Own, My Native Land. Toronto: The Ryerson Press, 1934.

Dennis, Clara. More About Nova Scotia: My Own, My Native Land. Toronto: The Ryerson Press, 1937.

Ducéré, Edouard. Dictionnaire Historique de Bayonne. Bayonne: Foltzer, 1911.

Ducéré, Edouard. Recherches Historiques Sur La Peche De La Morue Et La Decouverte De Terre-Neuve. Unknown: J. Emperauger, 1893. Accessed May 29, 2013. http://books.google.com/books?id=q-h5AAAAMAAJ&pg=PA28&dq=baleines+du cere+capbreton&hl=en&sa=X&ei=_rgCUuaWFsHwigL1-gCw&ved=0CDgQ6AEwAA#v=onepage&q=baleines%20ducere%20capbreton&f=false.

Fauteux, Aegidius. "La Baie de Cabarrus." Bulletin des Recherches Historiques 35 (February 1929): 72-74.

Fergusson, Charles Bruce. "Cabot's Landfall." Dalhousie Review 33 (Winter 1953): 257-76.

Fergusson, Charles Bruce, ed. Uniacke's Sketches of Cape Breton and Other Papers Relating to Cape Breton Island. Halifax: The Public Archives of Nova Scotia, 1958.

Fischer, David Hackett. Champlain's Dream: The European Founding of North America. New York: Random House, 2008.

Fortier, Margaret. "The Cultural Landscape of 18th Century Louisbourg." Accessed March 29, 2013. http://fortress.cbu.ca/search/MicroRS83_14.html.

Gray, Mildred. "Personal Letter from Canadian Department of Transport." Personal Communication, July 1, 2013.

Histoire Locale et Genealogie de la Cote Sud des Landes. "Cabarrus Family History." Accessed July 5 2013. http://www.cotesudmemoirevive.com/templates/cotesudmemoirevive.php.

Hornsby, S. J.. Nineteenth-Century Cape Breton: A Historical Geography. Montreal:

McGill-Queen's University Press, 1992.

Hutchings, J.A., and R.A. Myers. "The Biological Collapse of Atlantic Cod Off Newfoundland and Labrador: An Exploration of Historical Changes in Exploitation, Harvesting Technology, and Management." In The North Atlantic Fishery: Strengths, Weaknesses, and Challenges, edited by R. Arnason and L.F. Felt, 37-93. Charlottetown, PEI: Institute of Island Studies University of Prince Edward Island, 1995.

Kurlansky, Mark. Cod: A Biography of the Fish That Changed the World. New York: Penguin Books, 1997.

Larson, Eric. Thunderstruck. New York: Crown Publishing, 2006.

Lavery, M. and G. Lavery. Tides and Times: Life on the Cape Breton Coast at Gabarus and Vicinity, 1713-1990. Scarborough: Private Printer, 1991.

LeHuenen, Joseph. "The Role of the Basque, Breton and Norman Cod Fishermen in the Discovery of North America from the XVIth to the End of the XVIIIth Century." Arctic 37 (DECEMBER 1984): 520-527.

Lopez, Barry. "The Whaleboat: It's Surprising How Far a Ten-inch Craft Can Carry You." Outside Magazine (May 1998). Accessed July 14, 2013. http://www.outsideonline.com/outdoor-adventure/The-Whaleboat.html.

Lotz, P., and J. Lotz. Cape Breton Island. Vancouver: Douglas, David, and Charles, 1974.

MacGillivray, D., and B. Tennyson, eds.. Cape Breton Historical Essays. Sydney: College of Cape Breton Press, 1980.

McCord Museum of Canadian History. "Tradition, Change and Survival: Mi'Kmaq Tourist Art." Accessed July 7, 2013. http://www.mccord-museum.qc.ca/en/keys/webtours/tourID/VQ_P1_3_EN.

McLennan, J.S. Louisbourg From Its Foundation To Its Fall, 1713-1758. Halifax: The Book Room Limited, 1990.

Melville, Herman. Moby Dick; or, The White Whale. Boston: St. Botolph Society, 1892.

Menk, T. and E. Kersey. "Naming of Gabarus." Paper presented at the annual meeting for the Canadian Society for the Study of Names, Montreal, Quebec on May 30, 2010.

Menk, T. "Reasons for Gabarus's Population Growth." E-mail message to author, September 2, 2013.

Moore, Christopher. Louisbourg Portraits: Five Dramatic True Tales of People Who Lived in an Eighteenth Century Garrison Town. Toronto: McClelland & Stewart Ltd., 1982.

Morgan, Robert J. Early Cape Breton: From Founding to Famine. Wreck Cove: Breton Books, 2000.

Morgan, Robert J. Rise Again! The Story of Cape Breton Island. Book One. Wreck Cove: Breton Books, 2008.

Morgan, Robert J. Rise Again! The Story of Cape Breton Island from 1900 to Today. Book Two. Wreck Cove: Breton Books, 2009.

Nova Scotia Community Counts. "Census of Population 2001, 2006, and 2011." Accessed April 7, 2013. http://www.gov.ns.ca/finance/communitycounts/profiles/community/default.asp?gnum=com1722&gview=2&glevel=com.

Osborne, Harold S. Biographical Memoir of Alexander Graham Bell: 1847-1922. Vol. XXIII. Washington: Literary Licensing, 1943. Accessed February 28, 2013. http://books.nap.edu/html/biomems/abell.pdf.

Parker, John P. Cape Breton Ships and Men. London: George J. McLeod Limited, 1967.

Parkman, Francis. A Half Century of Conflict, France and England in North America. Volume II. Boston: Little, Brown, and Company, 1897.

Parks Canada. "Marconi National Historic Site of Canada." Accessed February 16, 2013. http://www.pc.gc.ca/eng/lhn-nhs/ns/marconi/natcul.aspx.

Poliandri, Simone. First Nations, Identity, and Reserve Life: The Mi'kmaq of Nova Scotia. Lincoln: University of Nebraska Press, 2011.

Prins, Harald E.L. The Mi'kmaq: Resistance, Accommodation, and Cultural Survival. New York: Harcourt Brace College Publishers, 1996.

Rousseau, Jacques. "Cabarrus." Bulletin des Recherches Historiques 46 (July 1940): 213-214.

Sherwood, K. "Number of Boats Fishing Out of Gabarus." Personal Communication, August 27, 2013.

Soulaire, Jacques. Les Baleines Franches: Kronos N°65. Paris: Editions L'Harmattan, 2012. Accessed August 7, 2013. http://books.google.com/books?id=Izql54mzKR4C&pg=PA121&lpg=PA121&dq=baleines+ducere&source=bl&ots=8vi36aUUbF&sig=Gf_9q78ST5CkVwXIP69PN52G5VA&hl=en&sa=X&ei=x7UCUpGHNsPKiwLV9oDoDQ&ved=0CEEQ6AEwBA#v=onepage&q=baleines%20ducere&f=false.

Taber, Jane. "For a Nova Scotia Fishing Village, There's Danger of Falling into the Ocean." The Globe and Mail, April 29, 2013.

Tennyson, Brian Douglas. Cape Bretoniana: An Annotated Bibliography. Toronto: University of Toronto Press, 2005.

Tennyson, Brian Douglas, ed. Impressions of Cape Breton. Sydney: University College of Cape Breton Press, 1986.

Unit Conversion. "A League." Accessed April 14, 2013. http://www.unitconversion.org/length/league-conversion.html%20accessed%20on%20april%2014.

United States. Navy Department, Hydrographic Office. Nova Scotia Pilot: Bay of Fundy, Southeast Coast of Nova Scotia and Coast of Cape Breton Island. . Washington: U.S. Government Printing Office, 1918. Accessed March 8, 2013. http://books.google.com/books?id=Vm0DAAAAYAAJ&pg=PA430&dq=temperate+industrious+and+thriving+people+gabarus&hl=en&sa=X&ei=F8_cUYucHOKrigLu9IDYDQ&ved=0CDUQ6AEwAQ#v=onepage&q=temperate%20industrious%20and%20thriving%20people%20gabarus&f=false.

Vernon, Charles William. Cape Breton, Canada. Toronto: Nation Publishing Company, 1903.

Wikimapia. "Gabarus Wilderness Area." Accessed March 23, 2013. http://wikimapia.org/9852354/Gabarus-Wilderness-Area.

Witham, J. "Grant Family Tree." Personal Communication, July 1, 2013.

Acknowledgements

There is no end to my thanks for the whole-hearted and generous support of Mildred Gray ("Mid") who was always happy to share over the course of our many conversations. Her own words tell the story of her admirable character and thoughtful assessment of more than nine decades of her life. Thank you Mid! So many family members gave their support including Nancy, Wayne, and Fred Dickie, Ken and June Grant, Albert and Marilyn Gray, Faye Libbey, and Sandra and Allister MacDonald. All Grant and Gray family members welcomed the book with open arms including cousins Linda Bagnell Besse and Lily Cann who also assisted with historic source material. Much appreciation goes to Jennifer Witham for her enthusiasm for the book and extraordinary expertise on the genealogy of the Grant Family. I express my gratitude to Evelyn Hunt who generously shared her collection of books about Gabarus and Cape Breton history, references that proved essential to the *Highlights of Gabarus History* section.

Florence Nygaard not only contributed her careful reading and editing skills, but directly facilitated Mrs. Gray's final review of the text and itemized the final edits for me. Alfie [Shih-Tzu] Nygaard further supported the effort with his loving companionship and eagerness for the many walks back and forth to Mrs. Gray's home. Many thanks to Florence for her unending goodwill and assistance in bringing this book into existence.

Grateful appreciation to Tim Menk and Gene Kersey who have been an instrumental source of ideas and encouragement. Their comprehensive investigation of the place name Gabarus is appreciatively referenced. Thanks are also due Rhodena Clark, a self-taught historian with over 60 years of gathering facts, figures, and stories about Gabarus. Her particular interest in explaining the origin of the name Gabarus set Tim and Gene on the trail to their research, and she has generously entrusted them as the guardians of her research and historic archives.

No publication of mine would be possible without the stalwart support and thoughtful and good-humored review of my sister Margot Scheuren who is always ready to infuse her intelligence and can find a typo anywhere in the cosmos of the written word. I always feel and honor the loving emotional presence of my children Jessie, Ben and Nate in anything I do. My friend Emily Jenkins has also well earned her credentials as a most excellent reviewer as have my other first readers Valerie Rauluk, Carol Carpenter and Pat Cook. I am very grateful for their great help and excellent input. Merci encore to my childhood friend Rusty Park who rescued me from making mistakes in my French translation of Cabarrus family history. Although we once shared a French class over fifty years ago, his French language skills have far surpassed my own. My friend Pierre Landau also helped me with the French language texts, so that I could better comprehend those sources, especially the ones on the history of Basque whaling and cod fishing. I very much appreciate the generous and talented artists who brought this book to tangible life. Hearty thanks to Carla Turco for her inviting and wonderful book design and maps, to Benjamin Schwartz for his boat drawings so evocative of another time, and to David "Fitz" Fitzsimmons for his delightful hand-drawn map of Gabarus Village.

I am especially grateful for the outstanding scholarly counsel and constructive critique of Dr. Brian Tennyson and Dr. James O. St. Clair and the helpful information provided by marine biologist Dr. Jeffrey Hutchings. The generous nature of Canadian scholars is extraordinary and much appreciated. Many thanks to the very knowledgeable and helpful staff of the Beaton Institute at Cape Breton University: Catherine Arseneau, Jane Arnold, Anne Marie MacNeil, and Gerardette Brown for their supportive interest and assistance with the tasks involved in utilizing photographic images from their collection. Sincere thanks to scholar Vanessa Childs Rolls who added her expertise to ensure that my endnotes and bibliography were correct. Appreciation to Tom Ayers, Director of Editorial at Cape Breton Post, for his support for utilizing the Cape Breton Post–published photograph by Vince Riley of the wreck of the Marshall Frank and to Blaise Abbass at Abbass Studios (1985) Ltd. who readily shared his father John's photo of the wreck of the Iceland II. I express my gratitude to Warren Gordon of Warren Gordon Photographic who so helpfully shared his beautiful aerial photograph of Gabarus Village.

My gratitude to Jocelyn Bethune who expressed her enthusiastic interest and kindly gave us permission to use one of her photographs from a story she wrote on Mrs. Gray in the Chronicle Herald. Best thanks to Jamie Whitters from Cape Breton Regional Municipality who sent me the latest maps of Gabarus to use as a reference for those included here. Much appreciation to Jacqueline Holmes and Tim White of Rising Tide Expeditions who contributed both steady support and permission to reproduce two of their photographs. Many thanks to Lillian and Kathy Harriss for always being ready to help in any way and for the wonderful picture of the Gray Family and their ice boat.

There isn't a person in Gabarus who didn't give smiling support to the effort to capture Mrs. Gray's oral history. Gwen Wheaton was mindful of when to visit Mrs. Gray, so as "not to interrupt the interview process." During our interviews, Shauna Hardy and Mary Gatto were so often a poised presence in Mrs. Gray's home. Dan and Diane Harris provided valuable perspectives on Gabarus history and ideas for further questions. Neighbor and fisherman Ken Sherwood kindly reviewed the sections on shallops and fishing methodologies. There are so many others. Truly, recording Mrs. Gray's recollections over the past three years always felt like a community effort. Best thanks to all.

Virtually every subject mentioned in the *Highlights of Gabarus History* invites further study and dialogue. I have gratefully relied on the comprehensive and wide-ranging work of previous researchers. In particular, several sources on Cape Breton history have been extensively referenced including the work of historians Brian Douglas Tennyson, Robert J. Morgan, George and Mary Lavery, and Ronald Caplan of Breton Books and *Cape Breton's Magazine*. I encourage using the endnotes and bibliography as a resource for delving further into the fascinating history of Gabarus, the place and its people. I take full responsibility for any mistakes and welcome comments and questions.

Claire E. Scheuren

CLAIRE E. SCHEUREN.
PHOTO BY BELATHÉE
PHOTOGRAPHY.
USED WITH PERMISSION.

Claire E. Scheuren is an American nonprofit executive, editor and author. Ms. Scheuren has been recognized with numerous public service honors in the U.S. including the American Institute for Public Service Jefferson Award for her work on human rights and citizen education issues. She edited six editions of the Reporter's Source Book for Project Vote Smart and is the creator of the 1992 *Campaign Game* which was syndicated nationally in over one hundred daily newspapers across the U.S. by the National Student/Parent Mock Election. Ms. Scheuren serves as Deputy Director of the Pima Prevention Partnership, a U.S.-award-winning nonprofit human service agency. Ms. Scheuren holds an M.A. in Organizational Leadership from Gonzaga University. Since 2008, Ms. Scheuren has been a resident of both Tucson, Arizona, and Gabarus, Nova Scotia.

CPSIA information can be obtained at www.ICGtesting.com
Printed in the USA
BVOW03s1634191113

336632BV00003BA/4/P